The Believer's Secret of Waiting on God

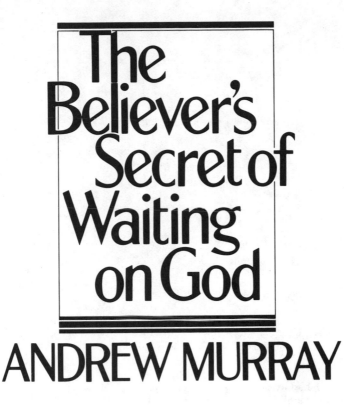

The Believer's Secret of Waiting on God

ANDREW MURRAY

BETHANY HOUSE PUBLISHERS
MINNEAPOLIS, MINNESOTA 55438
A Division of Bethany Fellowship, Inc.

Originally titled *Waiting on God*.

Copyright © 1986
Bethany House Publishers
All Rights Reserved

Published by Bethany House Publishers
A Division of Bethany Fellowship, Inc.
6820 Auto Club Road, Minneapolis, Minnesota 55438

Printed in the United States of America

Library of Congress Cataloging-in-Publication Data

Murray, Andrew, 1828-1917.
   The believer's secret of waiting on God.

   (Andrew Murray Christian maturity library)
   Rev. ed. of: Waiting on God.
   1. Trust in God—Christianity. I. Murray, Andrew, 1828-
1917. Waiting on God. II. Title. III. Series.
BV4637.M795   248.4   85-32068
ISBN 0-87123-886-1 (pbk.)

Books by Andrew Murray

ANDREW MURRAY CHRISTIAN MATURITY LIBRARY

The Believer's Absolute Surrender
The Believer's Call to Commitment
The Believer's Full Blessing of Pentecost
The Believer's New Covenant
The Believer's New Life
The Believer's Secret of Holiness
The Believer's Secret of Living Like Christ
The Believer's Secret of Obedience
The Believer's Secret of a Perfect Heart
The Spirit of Christ

ANDREW MURRAY PRAYER LIBRARY

The Believer's Prayer Life
The Believer's School of Prayer
The Ministry of Intercessory Prayer
The Secret of Believing Prayer

ANDREW MURRAY DEVOTIONAL LIBRARY

The Believer's Daily Renewal
The Believer's Secret of Waiting on God
Day by Day with Andrew Murray

How to Raise Your Children for Christ
Jesus Christ: Prophet-Priest
The Master's Indwelling
Money

ANDREW MURRAY was born in South Africa in 1828. After receiving his education in Scotland and Holland, he returned to that land and spent many years there as both pastor and missionary. He was a staunch advocate of biblical Christianity. He is best known for his many devotional books.

"Wait Thou Only Upon God"

"My soul, wait thou only upon God" (Ps. 62:5).
"What he hath prepared for him that waiteth for him" (Isa. 64:4).

"Wait only upon God"; my soul, be still,
And let thy God unfold His perfect will.
Thou fain would'st follow Him throughout this year,
Thou fain with listening heart His voice would hear,
Thou fain would'st be a passive instrument
Possessed by God, and ever Spirit-sent
Upon His service sweet—then be thou still,
For only thus can He in thee fulfill
His heart's desire. Oh, hinder not His hand
From fashioning the vessel He hath planned.
"Be silent unto God," and thou shalt know
The quiet, holy calm He doth bestow
On those who wait on Him; so shalt thou bear
His presence, and His life and light e'en where
The night is darkest, and thine earthly days
Shall show His love, and sound His glorious praise.
And He will work with hand unfettered, free,
His high and holy purposes through thee.
First *on* thee must that hand of power be turned,
Till in His love's strong fire thy dross is burned,
And thou come forth a vessel for thy Lord,

So frail and empty, yet, since He hath poured
Into thine emptiness His life, His love,
Henceforth through thee the power of God shall move
And He will work *for* thee. Stand still and see
The victories thy God will gain for thee;
So silent, yet so irresistible,
Thy God shall do the thing impossible.
Oh, question not henceforth what thou canst do;
Thou canst do *nought*. But He will carry through
The work where human energy had failed
Where all thy best endeavors had availed
Thee nothing. Then, my soul, wait and be still;
Thy God shall work for thee His perfect will.
If thou wilt take no less, *His best* shall be
Thy portion now and through eternity.

Freda Hanbury

Extract from
Address in Exeter Hall
May 31, 1895

Nothing has surprised me more than the letters that have come to me from missionaries and others around the world, devoted men and women, testifying to the need they feel in their work for a deeper and a clearer insight into all that Christ can be to them. Let us look to God to reveal himself among His people in a measure very few have realized. Let us expect great things of our God. At all our conventions and assemblies too little time is given to *waiting on God*. Is He not willing to put things right in His own divine way? Has the life of God's people reached the furthest limit of what God is willing to do for them? Surely not. We want to wait on Him; to put away our experiences, however blessed they have been; our conceptions of truth, however sound and scriptural we think they seem; our plans, however needful and suitable they appear; and give God time and place to show us what He can do, what He will do. God has new developments and new resources. He can do new things, unheard of things, hidden things. Let us enlarge our hearts and not limit Him. "When you came down, you did terrible things we had looked not for; the mountains flowed down at your presence."

Andrew Murray

Contents

Preface 13
1. The God of Our Salvation 15
2. The Keynote of Life 19
3. The True Place of the Creature 23
4. For Supplies 27
5. For Instruction 31
6. For All Saints 35
7. A Plea in Prayer 39
8. Strong and of Good Courage 43
9. With the Heart 47
10. In Humble Fear and Hope 51
11. Patiently 55
12. Keeping His Ways 59
13. For More Than We Know 63
14. The Way to the New Song 67
15. For His Counsel 71
16. And His Light in the Heart 75
17. In Times of Darkness 79
18. To Reveal Himself 83
19. As a God of Judgment 87
20. Who Waits on Us 91
21. The Almighty One 95
22. Its Certainty of Blessing 99
23. For Inconceivable Things 103

24. To Know His Goodness 107
25. Quietly 111
26. In Holy Expectancy 115
27. For Redemption 119
28. For the Coming of His Son 123
29. For the Promise of the Father 127
30. Continually 131
31. Only on God 135
Note 139

Preface

Before I left home for England, I had been very much impressed by the thought of how, in all our Christian life, personal and public, we need more of God. I had felt that we needed to train our people in their worship to wait on God, and to make the cultivation of a deeper sense of His presence, of more direct contact with Him, of entire dependence on Him, a definite aim of our ministry. In my message given in Exeter Hall, I expressed this simple thought in connection with all our Christian work. As I have already said, I was surprised at the response. I saw that God's Spirit had been working the same desire in many hearts.

The experiences of the past year, both personal and public, have greatly deepened the conviction. It is as if I am only beginning to see the deepest truth concerning God, and our relationship to Him, centered on waiting on God, and how very little, in our life and work, we have been sensitive to this need. The following pages are the outcome of my conviction, and of my desire to direct the attention of all believers to the one great remedy for all our needs. More than half of these chapters were written while on board a ship. I fear they bear the marks of being

13

somewhat crude and hasty. I have felt that I should write them over again. But I cannot do this now. And so I send them out with the prayer that He who loves to use the weak may give His blessing with them.

I do not know if it will be possible for me to put into a few words the chief things we need to learn. In a note on William Law at the close of this book, I have mentioned some. But what I want to say here is this: The great lack of our Christianity today is, *we do not know God.* The answer to every complaint of weakness and failure, the message to every congregation or convention seeking instruction on holiness, should simply be, What is the matter: *Where is your God?* If you really believe in God, He will put it all right. God is willing and able by His Holy Spirit. Stop expecting the solution from yourself, or the answer from anything there is in man, and simply yield yourself completely to God to work in you. He will do it all for you.

How simple this looks! And yet this is the gospel we know so little about. I feel ashamed as I send forth these very defective meditations; I can only cast them on the love of my brethren and of our God. May He use them to draw us to himself, to learn in practice and experience the blessed art of *waiting only on God.* Pray to God that we might get some right conception of what influence could be made by a life spent, not in thought, or imagination, or effort, but in the power of the Holy Spirit, wholly waiting upon God.

With my greeting in Christ to all God's saints it has been my privilege to meet, and no less to those I have not met, I offer myself, your brother and servant.

Andrew Murray

1

The God of Our Salvation

"Truly my soul waiteth upon God [*is silent unto God,* A.S.V.]: *from him cometh my salvation"* (Ps. 62:1).

If salvation indeed comes from God, and is entirely His work, just as our creation was, it follows that our first and highest duty is to wait on Him to do the work that pleases Him. Waiting then becomes the only way to experience full salvation, the only way to truly know God as the God of our salvation. All the difficulties that are brought forward, keeping us back from full salvation, have their cause in this one thing: our lack of knowledge and practice of waiting on God. All that the church and its members need for the manifestation of the mighty power of God in the world is the return to our true place, the place that belongs to us, both in creation and redemption, the place of absolute and unceasing dependence on God. Let us strive to see what the elements are that make up this most blessed and needful waiting on God. It may help us to look into the reasons why this grace is so neglected and to feel how infinitely desirable it is that the church, that is we believers, should learn this blessed secret at any price.

The deep need for this waiting on God lies equally in the nature of man and in the nature of God. God, as creator, formed man to be a vessel in which He could show forth His power and goodness. Man was not to have in himself a fountain of life, or strength, or happiness. The ever-living and only living One was intended each moment to be the communicator to man of all that he needed. Man's glory and blessedness was not to be independent, or dependent upon himself, but dependent on a God of such infinite riches and love. Man was to have the joy of receiving every moment out of the fullness of God. This was his blessed state as an unfallen creature.

When he turned from God, he was still absolutely dependent on Him. There was not the slightest hope of his recovery from the state of death, except in God, His power and mercy. It is God alone who began the work of redemption. It is God alone who continues and carries it on each moment in each individual believer. Even in the regenerate man there is no power of goodness in himself. He has and can have nothing except what he each moment receives while waiting on God. This is indispensable, and must be just as continuous and unbroken, as the breathing that maintains his natural life.

Because believers do not know their relationship to God of absolute poverty and helplessness, they have no sense of the need of absolute and unceasing dependence, or the unspeakable blessedness of continual waiting on God. But once a believer begins to see it, and consent to it, he by the Holy Spirit begins each moment to receive what God each moment works. Waiting on God becomes his brightest hope and joy. As he understands how God, as God, as infinite love, delights to impart His own nature to His child as fully as He can, how God is not weary of each moment keeping charge of his life and strength, he wonders how he ever thought otherwise of God than as a God to be waited on all day long. God unceasingly gives and works as His child unceasingly waits and receives. This is the blessed life.

"Truly my soul waiteth upon God: from him cometh my salvation." First we wait on God for salvation. Then we learn that salvation is only to bring us to God, and teach us to wait on Him. Then we find what is better still, that waiting on God is itself the highest salvation. It is ascribing to Him the glory of being all; it is experiencing that He is all to us. May God teach us the blessedness of waiting on Him!

My soul, wait only on God!

2

The Keynote of Life

"I have waited for thy salvation, O Lord" (Gen. 49:18).

It is not easy to say in exactly what sense Jacob used these words that appear in the midst of his prophecies regarding the future of his sons. But they do certainly indicate that both for himself and for them his expectation was from God alone. It was God's salvation he waited for, a salvation God had promised and which God alone could work out. Jacob knew he and his sons were under God's charge. Jehovah the everlasting God would show in them what His saving power is and does. The words point forward to that wonderful history of redemption which is not yet finished, and to the glorious future in eternity where the redemption is leading. They suggest to us how there is no salvation but God's salvation, and how waiting on God for it, whether for our personal experience or the world around us, is our first duty, our true source of blessing.

Let us think of ourselves and the inconceivably glorious salvation God has accomplished for us in Christ, and is now purposing to work out and perfect in us by His Spirit. Let us meditate until we begin to realize that every participation in this great salvation, from one moment to the next, must be the work of God himself. God cannot part with His grace, or goodness, or strength, as an external thing that He gives us, in the same way He gives the raindrops from heaven. No, He can only give it, and we can only enjoy it, as He works it directly and unceasingly. And the only reason He does not work it more effectually and continuously is that we do not let Him. We hinder Him either by our indifference or by our self-effort, so that He cannot do what He desires. What He asks of us, in the way of surrender, obedience, desire, and trust, is all comprised in this one phrase: waiting on Him, waiting for His salvation. It combines the deep sense of our entire helplessness to work what is divinely good, and our perfect confidence that God will work it all by His divine power.

Again, I say, let us meditate on the divine glory of the salvation God purposes to work out in us, until we know the truths it implies. Our heart is the scene of a divine operation more wonderful than creation. We can do as little toward the work as toward creating the world, except as God works in us to will and to do. God only asks us to yield, to consent, to wait on Him, and He will do it all. Let us meditate and be still until we see how proper and right and blessed it is that God alone does all. Then our soul will sink down in deep humility to say, "I have waited for thy salvation, O Lord." And the deep blessed background of all our praying and working will be: "Truly my soul waiteth upon God."

The application of the truth to wider circles, to those we labor among or intercede for, to the church of Christ around us, or throughout the world, is not difficult. There can be no good except what God works; to wait on God, and have the heart filled with faith in His working, and in that faith to pray for His mighty power to come down, is our only wisdom. Oh, for the eyes of our heart to be opened to see God working in ourselves and in others, and to see how blessed it is to worship and simply wait for His salvation!

Our private and public prayer is our chief expression of our relationship to God. It is mainly in them that our waiting on God must be exercised. If our waiting begins by quieting the activities of daily life, and being still before God; if we bow and seek to see God in His universal and almighty operation; if we yield to Him in the assurance that He is working and will work in us; if we maintain the place of humility and stillness, and surrender until God's Spirit has stirred up in us confidence that He will perfect His work, our waiting will indeed become the strength and the joy of the soul. Life will become one deep blessed cry: "I have waited for thy salvation, O Lord."

My soul, wait only on God!

3

The True Place of the Creature

"These wait all upon thee; that thou mayest give them their meat in due season. That thou givest them they gather: thou openest thine hand, they are filled with good" (Ps. 104:27, 28).

This psalm, in praise of the Creator, has been speaking of the birds and the beasts of the forest; of the young lions, and man going forth to his work; of the great sea, in which there are innumerable creeping organisms, both small and large. And it sums up the whole relationship of all creation to its Creator, and its continuous and universal dependence on Him in the one phrase: "These all wait upon thee!" Just as much as it was God's work to create, it is His work to maintain. As little as the creature could create itself, is it left to provide for itself. The whole creation is ruled by the one unalterable law of *waiting on God!*

The phrase is the simple expression of the very reason for which the creature was brought into existence, the very foundation of its constitution. The one purpose for which God gave life to creatures was that in them He might prove and show forth His wisdom, power, and

23

goodness, in His being each moment their life and happiness, and in pouring out to them, according to their capacity, the riches of His goodness and power. And just as this is the very place and nature of God, to be unceasingly the supplier of everthing the creature needs, so the very place and nature of the creature is nothing but this: to wait on God and receive from Him what He alone can give, what He delights to give.*

If through this book we hope to grasp what *waiting on God* is to be to the believer, to practice it and to experience its blessing, it is necessary for us to begin at the very beginning and see the deep reasonableness of the call that comes to us. We will come to understand how the duty is not an arbitrary command. We will see how it is not only made necessary by our sin and helplessness. It is simply and truly our restoration to our original destiny and our highest rank, to our true place and glory as creatures happily dependent on the all-glorious God.

If our eyes are once opened to this precious truth, all nature will become a preacher, reminding us of the relationship which was founded in creation and is now taken up in grace. As we read this psalm and learn to look on all life in nature as continually maintained by God, waiting on God will be seen as the greatest need of our being. As we think of the young lions and the ravens crying to Him, of the birds and the fishes and every insect waiting on Him, till He gives them their meat in due season, we will see that the very nature and glory of God is that He is a God who is to be waited on. Every thought of what nature is and what God is will give new force to the call: "Wait thou only upon God."

---

*See note on William Law on pp. 139–140.

"These wait all upon thee; that thou mayest *give*." It is God who gives all: let this truth enter deeply into our hearts. Until we fully understand all that is implied in our waiting on God, and until we have even been able to cultivate the habit, let the truth enter our souls. Waiting on God, unceasing and entire dependence upon Him, is, in heaven and earth, the only true religion. It is the one unalterable and all-comprehensive expression of our true relationship to the One in whom we live.

Let us resolve at once that it will be the one characteristic of our life and worship, to continually, humbly, and truthfully wait on God. We may rest assured that the One who made us for himself that He might give himself to us and in us, will *never* disappoint us. In waiting on Him we will find rest and joy and strength and the supply of every need.

My soul, wait only on God!

4

For Supplies

"The Lord upholdeth all that fall, and raiseth up all those that be bowed down. The eyes of all wait upon thee; and thou givest them their meat in due season" (Ps. 145:14, 15).

Psalm 104 is a psalm of creation, and the words "these wait all upon thee" were used with reference to the animal creation. Here we have a psalm of the kingdom, and "the eyes of all wait upon thee" point specifically to the needs of God's saints, of those who fall and are bowed down. What the universe and the animal creation does unconsciously, God's people are to do intelligently and voluntarily. Man is to be the interpreter of nature. He is to prove that there is nothing nobler or more blessed in the exercise of our free will than to use it in waiting on God.

If an army has been sent out to march into an enemy's country, and news is received that it is not advancing, the question is at once asked, what may be the cause of delay. The answer will very often be: "Waiting for supplies." If the stores of provisions or clothing or ammunition have not arrived, they dare not proceed.

27

It is no different in the Christian life: day by day, for every step, we need our supplies from above. And there is nothing so necessary as to cultivate that spirit of dependence on God and of confidence in Him which refuses to go on without the needed supply of grace and strength.

If the question is asked, whether this is different from what we do when we pray, the answer should be that there can be a lot of praying with very little waiting on God. In praying we are often occupied with ourselves, with our own needs, and our own efforts in the presentation of them. In waiting on God, the first thought is of *the God on whom we wait*. We enter His presence, and feel we need to simply be quiet, so that He, as God, can overshadow us with himself. God longs to reveal himself, to fill us with himself. Waiting on God gives Him time in His own way and divine power to come to us.

It is especially at the time of prayer that we ought to set ourselves to cultivate this spirit.

Before you pray, bow quietly before God, to remember and realize who He is, how near He is, how certainly He can and will help. Be still before Him and allow His Holy Spirit to waken and stir up in your soul the childlike disposition of absolute dependence and confident expectation. Wait on God as a living being, as the living God, who notices you and is longing to fill your every need. Wait on God till you know you have met Him; prayer will then become so different.

And when you are praying, let there be intervals of silence, reverent stillness of soul, in which you yield yourself to God, in case He may have something He wishes to teach you or to work in you. Waiting on Him will become the most blessed part of prayer, and the answer to your prayer will be twice as precious since it is the fruit of your fellowship with the Holy One. God has so ordained it, in harmony with His holy nature and with ours, that waiting on Him should be the honor we give Him. Let us bring Him the service gladly and truthfully. He will reward it abundantly.

"The eyes of all wait upon thee; and thou givest them their meat in due season." God provides in nature for the creatures He has made. How much more will He provide in grace for those He has redeemed! Learn to say about every want, every failure, and every lack of the grace you need: I have waited too little on God, or He would have given me in due season all I needed. And then say:

My soul, wait only on God!

5

For Instruction

"Show me thy ways, O Lord; teach me thy paths. Lead me in thy truth, and teach me: for thou art the God of my salvation; on thee do I wait all the day" (Ps. 25:4, 5).

I spoke about an army at the point of entering an enemy's territories whose reason for delay was: "Waiting for supplies." Their answer could also have been: "Waiting for instructions," or "Waiting for orders." If the last dispatch had not been received with the final orders of the commander in chief, the army would not have dared to move. It is the same in the Christian life—as deep as the need of *waiting for supplies* is the need of *waiting for instructions*.

See how beautifully this comes out in Psalm 25. The writer knew and loved God's laws supremely, and meditated in that law day and night. But he knew this was not enough. He knew that for the right spiritual grasping of the truth, and for the right personal application of it to his own circumstances, he needed a direct divine teaching.

The psalm has always been a very peculiar one because of the repeated expression of the author's need for divine teaching, and the childlike confidence that it would be given. Study the psalm until your heart is filled with two thoughts: the absolute need and the absolute certainty of divine guidance. It is with these thoughts in mind that he declares: "On thee do I wait all the day." Waiting for guidance, waiting for instruction, all the day, is a very blessed part of waiting on God.

The Father in heaven is so interested in His child, and so longs to have his life in step with His will and His love, that He is willing to keep the child's guidance entirely in His own hand. He knows so well that we do not do what is really holy and heavenly, except when He works it in us, that He intends His very demands to become promises of what He will do, in watching over and leading us all day long. We may count on Him to teach us *His* way and show us *His* path not only in special trials and hard times, but in everyday life.

And what is needed in us to receive this guidance? Waiting for instructions, waiting on God. "On thee do I wait all the day." We want in our times of prayer to give clear expression to our sense of need and our faith in His help. We want to become fully conscious of our ignorance about what God's way may be and our need of the divine light shining within us if our way is to become like the sun, shining more and more brightly as it approaches high noon. And we want to wait quietly before God in prayer until the deep, restful assurance fills us. It will be given—"the meek will he guide in the way."

"On thee do I wait all the day." The special surrender to divine guidance in our prayer time must cultivate, and be followed up by, the habitual looking upward "all the day." As simple as it is, to one who has eyes, to walk all day in the light of the sun, so simple and delightful can it become to a soul that has practiced waiting on God, to walk all day in the enjoyment of God's light and leading. What is needed to help us find such a life is one thing: the real knowledge and faith of God as the only source of wisdom and goodness, as always ready and longing to be to us all that we can possibly need. Yes, this is the one thing we need! If only we could see our God in His love, if only we believed that He waits to be gracious, that He waits to be our life and to work His will in us—how this waiting on God would become our highest joy, the natural and spontaneous response of our hearts to His great love and glory!

My soul, wait only on God!

6

For All Saints

"Let none that wait on thee be ashamed" (Ps. 25:3).

In our meditation for today, let each one of us forget himself and think of the great number of God's people, saints throughout the world, who are at this time waiting on Him. And let us all join in this fervent prayer for each other: "Let none that wait on thee be ashamed."

Just think for a moment of the multitude of people who need that prayer; how many there are who are sick and weary and alone, to whom it seems as if their prayers are not answered, and who sometimes begin to fear that their hope is in vain. And then remember the many servants of God, ministers or missionaries, teachers or workers, whose hopes in their work have been disappointed, and whose longing for power and blessing remains unsatisfied. And then, too, think of how many have heard of a life of rest and perfect peace, of abiding light and fellowship, of strength and victory, but who cannot find the path. In each of these cases, there is no explanation but that they have not yet learned the secret of fully waiting on God. They simply need, what we all need, the living assurance that waiting on God

35

can never be in vain. Let us remember those who are in danger of fainting or being weary, and unite in the cry, "Let none that wait on thee be ashamed!"

If this intercession for all who wait on God becomes part of our waiting on Him for ourselves, we shall help to bear each other's burdens and so fulfill the law of Christ.

There will be introduced into our waiting on God that element of unselfishness and love which is the path to the highest blessing and the fullest communion with God. Love to our neighbor and love to God are inseparably linked. In God, the love to His Son *and to us* are one: "That the love wherewith thou hast loved me may be in them." In Christ, the love of the Father to Him and *His love to us* are one: "As the Father loved me, so have I loved you." In us, He asks that His love to us be *ours* to our neighbor: "As I have loved you, that ye love one another." All the love of God and of Christ are inseparably linked with love to our neighbor. And how can we, day by day, prove and cultivate this love in any other way than by daily praying for each other? Christ did not seek to enjoy the Father's love for himself; He passed it all on to us. All true seeking of God, and His love for ourselves, will be inseparably linked with the thought and the love of our neighbor in prayer for them.

"Let none that wait on thee be ashamed." Twice in the psalm David speaks of his waiting on God for himself; here he thinks of *all* who wait on Him. Let this page carry the message to all God's tried and weary ones, that there are more people praying for them than they know. Let it stir them and us in our waiting to make a point of at times forgetting ourselves, and to enlarge our hearts and say to the Father: "*These all wait upon thee*, and thou givest them their meat in due season." Let it inspire us all with new courage—for who is there who is not at times ready to faint and be weary? "Let none that wait on thee be ashamed" is a promise in a prayer, "They that wait on thee shall not be ashamed!" From many, many people who have found out for themselves the cry comes to everyone who needs the help, "Wait on the Lord; be of good courage, and he shall strengthen your heart; wait, I say, on the Lord. Be of good courage, and he shall strengthen your heart, all ye that wait on the Lord."

Blessed Father, we humbly ask you, let none that wait on you be ashamed; no, not one. Some are weary, and the time of waiting appears long. And some are weak and scarcely know how to wait. And some are so entangled in the effort of their prayers and their work, they think that they can find no time to wait continually. Father, teach us all how to wait! Teach us to think of each other and pray for each other. Teach us to think of you, the God of all waiting ones. Father, let none that wait on you be ashamed! For Jesus' sake. Amen.

My soul, wait only on God!

7

A Plea in Prayer

"Let integrity and uprightness preserve me; for I wait on thee" (Ps. 25:21).

For the third time in this psalm we have the word *wait*. As before in verse 5, "On thee do I wait all the day," so it is here too, the believer appeals to God to remember that he is waiting on Him, looking for an answer. It is a great thing for a soul not only to wait on God, but to be filled with such a consciousness that its whole spirit and position is that of one who is waiting that it can, in childlike confidence, say, Lord, you know I am waiting on you! It will prove to be a mighty plea in prayer, one giving ever-increasing boldness of expectation to claim the promise: "They that wait on me shall not be ashamed!"

The prayer referred to in this plea, the one for which we are now waiting on God, is one of great importance in the spiritual life. If we draw near to God, it must be with a true heart. There must be perfect integrity and wholeheartedness in our dealing with God. As we read in the next psalm (26:1, 11): "Judge me, O Lord; for I have walked in mine integrity.... As for me, I will

walk in mine integrity," there must be perfect uprightness or single-heartedness before God, as it is written:
"His righteousness is for the upright in heart." The soul
must know that it allows for itself nothing sinful, nothing doubtful. If it is indeed to meet the Holy One and
receive His full blessing, it must be with a heart wholly
and singly given up to His will. The whole attitude that
propels us in the waiting must be, "Let integrity and
uprightness"—you see that I desire to come to you in
this way. You know I am looking to you to work them
perfectly in me—"preserve me; for I wait on thee."

And if at our first attempt to truly live the life of
fully and always waiting on God, we begin to discover
how much that perfect integrity is wanting, this will
be one of the blessings that comes from waiting. *A soul
cannot seek close fellowship with God, or attain the
abiding consciousness of waiting on Him all day long,
without a completely honest and entire surrender to all
His will.*

"For I wait on thee." It is not only in connection with
the prayer of our text but with every prayer that this
plea may be used. To use it often will be a great blessing
to ourselves. Let us therefore study the words well until
we know all that they mean. It must be clear to us *what
we are waiting for.* It may be waiting for God in our
times of prayer to take His place as God, and to work
in us the sense of His holy presence and nearness. It
may be a special petition to which we are expecting an
answer. It may be our whole inner life in which we are
on the lookout for God's giving of His power. It may be
the whole state of His church and saints, or some part
of His work, for which our eyes are ever toward Him.
It is good that we sometimes recount exactly what things
we are waiting for, and as we say definitely about each
of them, "On thee do I wait," we will be emboldened to

claim the answer, "*For* on thee do I wait."

It must also be clear to us *on whom we are waiting*. Not an idol, a god of whom we have made an image by our conceptions of what He is. No, it is the living God as He really is—in His great glory, His infinite holiness, His power, wisdom, and goodness, in His love and nearness. It is the presence of a beloved or a dreaded master that attracts the whole attention of the servant who waits on him. It is *the presence of God, as He can in Christ by His Holy Spirit both make himself known* and keep the soul under its covering and shadow, that will attract and strengthen the true waiting spirit. Let us be still and wait and worship till we know how near He is, and then say, "*On you do I wait.*"

And then, let it be very clear too that *we are waiting*. Let that become so much our consciousness that the utterance comes spontaneously, "On you *I do wait* all day long; *I wait* on you." This will indeed imply sacrifice and separation, a soul entirely given up to God as its all, its only joy. This waiting on God has hardly yet been acknowledged as the only true Christianity. And yet if it is true that God alone is goodness and joy and love; if it is true that our highest blessedness is in having as much of God as we can; if it is true that Christ has redeemed us wholly for God, and made a life of continual abiding in His presence possible, nothing less ought to satisfy than for our plea to be constantly, "I wait on you."

My soul, wait only on God!

8

Strong and of Good Courage

"Wait for the Lord; be strong, and let your heart take courage; yea, wait for the Lord" (Ps. 27:14, RSV).

The psalmist had just said, "I had fainted, unless I had believed to see the goodness of the Lord in the land of the living." If it had not been for his faith in God, his heart would have fainted. But in the confident assurance in God which faith gives, he urges himself and us to remember one thing above all—to wait on God. "Wait for the Lord: be strong, and let your heart take courage: yea, wait for the Lord." One of the greatest needs in our waiting on God, one of the deepest secrets of its blessedness and blessing, is a quiet, confident persuasion that it is not in vain; courage to believe that God will hear and help; we are waiting on a God who never could disappoint His people.

"Be strong and of good courage." These words are frequently found in connection with some great and difficult combat with the power of strong enemies, and the utter insufficiency of all human strength. Is waiting on God a work so difficult that such words are needed: "Be strong, and let your heart take courage"?

43

Yes, indeed. The deliverance for which we often have to wait is from enemies, in whose presence we are powerless. The blessings for which we plead are spiritual and all unseen; things impossible with men; heavenly, supernatural, divine realities. Our heart may well faint and fail. Our souls are so unaccustomed to holding fellowship with God. The God on whom we wait so often appears to hide himself. We who have to wait are often tempted to fear that we do not wait correctly, that our faith is too weak, that our desire is not as upright or as earnest as it should be, that our surrender is not complete. In the middle of all these causes of fear or doubt, what a blessing to hear the voice of God: "Wait on the Lord! Be strong, and let your heart take courage! Yea, wait for the Lord"! Let nothing in heaven or earth or hell keep you from waiting on your God in full assurance that it cannot be in vain.

The one lesson our text teaches us is this, that when we set ourselves to wait on God we should resolve beforehand that it will be with the most confident expectation of God's meeting and blessing us. We should make up our minds that nothing was ever so sure as that waiting on God will bring us untold and unexpected blessing. We are in such a habit of evaluating God and His work in us by *what we feel* that it is very likely that when we begin to further develop waiting on Him, we will be discouraged because we do not find any special blessing from it. The message comes to us: "Above everything, when you wait on God, do so in the spirit of abounding hopefulness. It is God in His glory, in His power, in His love longing to bless you that you are waiting on."

If you say you are afraid of deceiving yourself with false hope because you do not see or feel any valid reason for such special expectations, my answer is, It is

God who is the valid reason for your expecting great things. Oh, do learn the lesson! You are not going to wait on yourself to see what you feel and what changes come to you. You are going to WAIT ON GOD, to know *first* WHAT HE IS, and then after that, what He will do. The whole duty and blessedness of waiting on God has its root in this, that He is such a blessed being, full, to overflowing, of goodness and power and life and joy, that we, however wretched, cannot for any time come into contact with Him, without that life and power secretly, silently beginning to enter into us and blessing us. God is love! That is the one only and all-sufficient reason for your expectation. Love seeketh out its own: God's love is *His delight to impart himself and His blessedness* to His children. Come, and however weak you feel, just wait in His presence. As a weak, sickly invalid is brought out into the sunshine to let its warmth go through him, come with all that is dark and cold in you *into the sunshine of God's holy, omnipotent love,* and sit and wait there, with the one thought: Here I am, in the sunshine of His love. As the sun does its work in the weak one who seeks its rays, *God will do His work in you.* Oh, do trust Him fully! "Wait for the Lord! Be strong, and let your heart take courage! Yea, wait for the Lord!"

My soul, wait only on God!

9

With the Heart

"Be strong, and let your heart take courage, all you who wait for the Lord" (Ps. 31:24, RSV).

The words are nearly the same as in our last chapter. But I gladly take advantage of them again to press home a much-needed lesson for all who desire to learn truly and fully what waiting on God is. The lesson is this: It is *with the heart* we must wait on God. "Let *your heart* take courage." All our waiting depends on the state of the heart. As a man's heart is, so is he before God. We can advance no further or deeper into the holy place of God's presence to wait on Him there than our heart is prepared for it by the Holy Spirit. The message is: *"Let your heart* take courage, all you who wait for the Lord."

The truth appears to be so simple that some may ask, This is obvious, is it not? So what is the need of insisting on it so specifically? Because very many Christians have no sense of the great difference between the religion of the mind and the religion of the heart, and the former is far more diligently cultivated than the latter. They do not know how infinitely greater

47

the heart is than the mind. It is in this that one of the main causes must be found for weakness of our Christian life, and it is only as this is understood that waiting on God will bring its full blessing.

Proverbs 3:5 may help to make this point clear. Speaking of a life in the fear and favor of God, it says: "Trust in the Lord with all thine heart; and lean not unto thine own understanding." In all religion we have to use these two powers. The mind has to gather knowledge from God's Word and prepare the food by which the heart with the inner life is to be nourished. But here comes the terrible danger of our leaning on our own understanding and trusting in our apprehension of divine things. People imagine that if they give mental attention to the truth, the spiritual life will as a matter of course be strengthened. And this is by no means the case. The understanding deals with conceptions and images of divine things, but it cannot reach the real life of the soul. Hence the command: "Trust in the Lord with all thine heart, and lean not upon thine own understanding." It is with the heart man believes, and comes into touch with God. It is in the heart God has given His Spirit, to be there to us the presence and the power of God working in us. In all our religion it is the heart that must trust and love and worship and obey. My mind is completely unable to create or maintain the spiritual life within me. The heart must wait on God for Him to work it in me.

It is this way even in the physical life. My reason may tell me what to eat and drink, and how the food nourishes me. But in the eating and feeding, my reason can do nothing—the body has its organs for that special purpose. In the same way, reason may tell me what God's Word says, but it can do nothing for the feeding of the soul on the bread of life—this the heart alone can do by its faith and trust in God. A man may be studying the nature and effects of food or sleep; when he wants to eat or sleep he sets aside his thoughts and study, and uses the power of eating or sleeping. And so the Christian always needs, when he has studied or heard God's Word, to cease from his thoughts, to put no trust in them, and to waken up his heart to open itself before God, and seek the living fellowship with Him.

Here is the blessing of waiting on God: to confess the inability of all my thoughts and efforts, and to set myself to bow my heart before Him in holy silence, trusting Him to renew and strengthen His own work in me. And this is just the lesson of our text: "Let *your heart* take courage, all you who wait on the Lord." Remember the difference between knowing with the mind and believing with the heart. Beware of the temptation of leaning on your understanding, with its clear strong thoughts. They only help you to know what the heart must get from God—in themselves they are only images and shadows. "Let *your heart* take courage, all you who wait for the Lord." Present it before Him as that wonderful part of your spiritual nature in which God reveals himself and by which you can know Him. Develop the greatest confidence that though you cannot see into your heart, God is working there by His Holy Spirit. Let the heart wait at times in perfect silence and quiet; in its hidden depths God will work. Be sure of this, and simply wait on Him. Give your whole heart, with its secret workings, into God's hands continually. He wants the heart and takes it, and as God, dwells in it. "Be strong, and let your heart take courage, all you who wait for the Lord."

My soul, wait only on God!

10

In Humble Fear and Hope

"Behold, the eye of the Lord is upon them that fear him, upon them that hope in his mercy; to deliver their soul from death, and to keep them alive in famine. Our soul waiteth for the Lord: he is our help and our shield. For our heart shall rejoice in him, because we have trusted in his holy name. Let thy mercy, O Lord, be upon us, according as we hope in thee" (Ps. 33:18–22).

God's eye is on His people; their eye is on Him. In waiting on God, our eye, looking up to Him, meets His looking down on us. The blessedness of waiting on God is that it takes our eyes and thoughts away from ourselves, even our needs and desires, and occupies us with our God. We worship Him in His glory and love, with His all-seeing eye watching over us that He may supply our every need. Let us consider this wonderful meeting between God and His people, and carefully notice what we are taught here about those on whom God's eye rests, and about Him on whom *our* eye rests.

"The eye of the Lord is on them that *fear* him, on them that *hope* in his mercy." Fear and hope are generally thought to be in conflict with each other. In the presence and worship of God, they are found side by side in perfect and beautiful harmony. This is because in God all apparent contradictions are reconciled. Righteousness and peace, judgment and mercy, holiness and love, infinite power and infinite gentleness, a majesty that is exalted above all heaven and a condescension that bows very low, meet and kiss each other. There is indeed a fear involving punishment that is cast out entirely by perfect love. But there is a fear that is found in the very heavens. In the song of Moses and the Lamb they sang, "Who shall not fear thee, O Lord, and glorify thy name?" And out of the very throne the voice came: "Praise our God, all ye his servants, and ye that fear him." Let us in our waiting always seek "to fear the glorious and fearful name, the Lord thy God." The deeper we bow before His holiness in holy fear and adoring awe, in deep reverence and humble self-abasement, even as the angels veil their faces before the throne, the more will His holiness press on us and our souls be prepared to have God reveal himself. The deeper we enter into the truth that "no flesh glory in his presence" will we be permitted to see His glory. "The eye of the Lord is on them that fear him."

"On them that hope in his mercy." The true fear of God does not keep us from hope. On the contrary, it stimulates and strengthens hope. The lower we bow, the deeper we feel we have nothing to hope in but His mercy. The lower we bow, the nearer God will come, and make our hearts bold to trust Him. Let every exercise of waiting, our whole habit of waiting on God, be pervaded by abounding hope—a hope as bright and boundless as God's mercy. The fatherly kindness of God is such that, however we come to Him, we may confidently hope in His mercy.

Such are God's waiting ones. And now, think of the

God on whom we wait. "The eye of the Lord is on them that fear him, on them that hope in his mercy; to deliver their soul from death, and to keep them alive in famine." Not to prevent the *danger* of death and famine—this is often needed to stir up men to wait on Him—but to deliver and keep alive. For the dangers are often very real and dark; the situation, whether in the natural or spiritual life, may appear to be utterly hopeless. But there is always one hope: *God's eye is on them.*

That eye sees the danger, and in tender love sees His trembling waiting child. He sees the moment when the heart is ripe for the blessing and the way in which it is to come. This living, mighty God, oh, let us fear Him and hope in His mercy! And let us humbly but boldly say, "Our soul waiteth for the Lord; he is our help and our shield. Let thy mercy be upon us, O Lord, according as we hope in thee."

Oh, the blessedness of waiting on such a God! A God who is present to help in every time of trouble; a shield and defense against every danger. Children of God, will you not learn to sink down in entire helplessness and impotence and in stillness to wait and see the salvation of God? In the driest spiritual famine, and when death appears to have the upper hand, oh, wait on God! He does deliver, He does keep alive. Say this not only when you are alone, but say it to each other—the psalm speaks not of one but of God's people—"*Our* soul waiteth for the Lord: he is *our* help and *our* shield." Strengthen and encourage each other in the holy exercise of waiting, that each person may not only say of himself, but of his fellow believers, "*We* have waited for him; *we* will be glad and rejoice in his salvation."

My soul, wait only on God!

11

Patiently

"Rest in the Lord, and wait patiently for him. . . . Those that wait upon the Lord, they shall inherit the earth" (Ps. 37:7, 9).

"In patience possess your souls." "Ye have need of patience." "Let patience have its perfect work, that ye may be perfect and entire." Through words like these the Holy Spirit shows us what an important element in the Christian life and character patience is. And nowhere is there a better place for cultivating or displaying it than in waiting on God. There we discover how impatient we are and what our impatience means. We confess at times that we are impatient with men and circumstances that hinder us, or with ourselves and our slow progress in the Christian life. If we truly set ourselves to wait on God, we will find that it is with Him we are impatient, because He does not at once, or as soon as we would like, give us what we ask. It is in waiting on God that our eyes are opened to believe in His wise and sovereign will, and to see that the sooner and more completely we yield absolutely to it, the more surely His blessing can come to us.

55

"It is not of him that willeth, nor of him that runneth, but of God that showeth mercy." We have as little power to increase or strengthen our spiritual life as we had to originate it. We "were born not of the will of the flesh, nor of the will of man, but of the will of God." So, our willing and running, our desire and effort, accomplish nothing; what accomplishes is "of God that showeth mercy." All the exercises of the spiritual life—our reading and praying, our willing and doing—have their own great value. But they can go no further than this, that they point the way and prepare us in humility to look to and depend alone on God himself, and in patience to wait for His time and mercy. The waiting is to teach us our absolute dependence on God's mighty working, and to make us in perfect patience place ourselves at His disposal. They that wait on the Lord shall inherit the land: the promised land and its blessing. The heirs must wait; they can afford to wait.

"Rest in the Lord, and wait patiently for him." Scholars say that "rest in the Lord" may also be read, "Be silent to the Lord," or "Be still before the Lord." It is resting in the Lord, in His will, His promise, His faithfulness, and His love, that makes patience easy. And resting in Him is nothing but being silent to Him, still before Him. Having our thoughts and wishes, our fears and hopes, hushed into calm and quiet by that great peace of God which passes all understanding. That peace keeps the heart and mind when we are anxious for anything, because we have made our request known to Him. The rest, the silence, the stillness, the patient waiting—all find their strength and joy in God himself.

The need for patience, and the reasonableness and the blessedness of patience will be opened up to the waiting soul. Our patience will be seen to be the counterpart of God's patience. He longs to bless us far more than we can desire it. But as the farmer has great patience till the fruit is ripe, so God accommodates himself to our slowness and bears with us. Let us remember this and wait patiently. Of each promise and every answer to prayer the statement is true: "I the Lord will hasten it *in its time*."

"Rest in the Lord, and wait patiently for him." Yes, *for* Him. Seek not only the help or the gift, seek *Him*; wait for Him. Give God His glory by resting in Him, by trusting Him fully, by waiting patiently for Him. This patience honors Him greatly; it leaves Him, as God on the throne, to do His work; it yields self wholly into His hands. It lets God *be God*. If your waiting is for some special request, wait patiently. If your waiting is more the exercise of the spiritual life seeking to know and have more of God, wait patiently. Whether it is in the shorter specific periods of waiting or the continuous habit of the soul, rest in the Lord, be still before the Lord, and wait patiently. "They that wait on the Lord shall inherit the land."

My soul, wait only on God!

12

Keeping His Ways

"Wait on the Lord, and keep his way, and he shall exalt thee to inherit the land" (Ps. 37:34).

If we want to find a man we are longing to meet, we ask about the place and the way he is to be found. When waiting on God, we need to be very careful that we keep His ways; outside of these we can never expect to find Him. "Thou meetest him that rejoiceth and worketh righteousness; those that remember *thee in thy ways*." We may be sure that God can never be found except in His way. And in that way, by the soul who seeks and patiently waits, He is always to be found. "Wait on the Lord, and keep his way, and he shall exalt thee."

The connection is very close between the two parts of the command. "Wait on the Lord"—having to do with worship and attitude—"and keep his way"—dealing with walk and work. The outer life must be in harmony with the inner; the inner must be the inspiration and the strength for the outer. It is our God who has made known in His Word His way for our conduct, and invites our confidence that His grace and help will come to our hearts. If we do not keep His way, our waiting on Him

59

can bring no blessing. The surrender in full obedience to all His will is the secret of full access to all the blessings of His fellowship.

Notice how strongly this comes out in the psalm. It speaks of the evil man who prospers in his activities, and calls on the believer not to be disturbed. When we see men around us prosperous and happy while they forsake God's ways, and ourselves left in difficulty or suffering, we are in danger of first being troubled at what appears so unjust and then gradually yielding to seek our prosperity in *their* path. The psalm says: "Fret not thyself. . . . Trust in the Lord, and do good. . . . Rest in the Lord, and wait patiently for him. . . . Cease from anger, and forsake wrath. . . . Depart from evil, and do good. . . . The Lord . . . forsaketh not his saints. . . . The righteous shall inherit the land. . . . The law of his God is in his heart; none of his steps shall slide." And then follows (the phrase occurs for the third time in the psalm), "*Wait* on the Lord, *and keep his way*." Do what God asks you to do; God will do more than you can ask Him to do.

Do not have this fear: I cannot keep His way. It will rob you of your confidence. If you do not have the strength to keep all His ways, surrender yourself willingly and trustingly to God, and the strength will come in waiting on Him. Give your whole being to God without holding back and without doubting. He will prove himself to you, and work in you that which is pleasing in His sight through Jesus Christ. Keep His ways as you know them in the Word. Keep His ways, as nature teaches them, in always doing what appears right. Keep His ways as providence points them out. Keep His ways as the Holy Spirit suggests. Do not think of waiting on God while you say you are not willing to walk in His path. However weak you feel, only be willing, and He who has worked to *will*, will work to *do* by His power.

"Wait on the Lord, and keep his way." It may be that the consciousness of weakness and sin makes our text look more like a hindrance than a help in waiting on God. Don't let yourself think that way. We have said more than once that the starting point and groundwork of this waiting is utter and absolute powerlessness. So come with every temptation you feel in yourself, every memory of unwillingness, unwatchfulness, unfaithfulness, and all that causes your unceasing self-condemnation. Put your powerlessness in God's almighty power, and find in waiting on God your deliverance. Your failure has been because of only one thing. You tried to conquer and obey in your own strength. Come and bow before God until you learn that He is the God who alone is good, and alone can work any good thing. Believe that in yourself, and all that nature can do, there is no true power. Be content to receive from God each moment of the day His mighty grace and life, and waiting on God will become the renewal of your strength to run in His ways and not be weary, to walk in His paths and never faint. "Wait on the Lord, and keep his way" will be a command *and* promise in one.

My soul, wait only on God!

13

For More Than We Know

*"And now, Lord, what wait I for? my hope is in thee.
Deliver me from all my transgressions"* (Ps. 39:7, 8).

There may be times when we feel as if we do not
know what we are waiting for. There may be other times
when we think we do know, and it would be good for us
to realize that we do not know what to ask. God is able
to do for us immeasurably more than all we ask or
think, and we are in danger of limiting Him when we
confine our desires and prayers to our own thoughts. It
is a great thing at times to say, as our psalm says, "And
now, Lord, what wait I for?" That is, I hardly know or
can tell; I can only say this, "My hope is in thee."

We clearly see this limiting of God in the case of
Israel! When Moses promised them meat in the wilderness, they doubted, saying, Can God furnish a table
in the wilderness? He struck the rock and the water
gushed out. But can He also give us bread? Can He
provide meat for His people? If they had been asked
whether God could provide streams in the desert, they
would have answered yes. God had done it; He could do
it again. But when the thought came of God doing

63

something new, they limited Him. Their expectation could not rise beyond their past experience, or their own thoughts of what was possible. In the same way we may be limiting God by our conceptions of what He has promised or is able to do. Let us beware of limiting the Holy One of Israel by the way we pray. Let us believe that the very promises of God we claim have a divine meaning, infinitely beyond our thoughts of them. Let us believe that His fulfillment of them can be, in a power and an abundance of grace, beyond our farthest imagination. And then let us develop the habit of waiting on God, not only for what we think we need, but for all His grace and power are ready to do for us.

In every true prayer there are two hearts involved. The one is your heart, with its little, dark, human thoughts of what you need and what God can do. The other is God's great heart, with its infinite, its divine purposes of blessing. What do you think? To which of these should the larger place be given in your approach to Him? Undoubtedly, to the heart of God. Everything depends on knowing and being occupied with that. But how little this is done. This is what waiting on God is meant to teach you. Just think of God's wonderful love and redemption and the meaning these words must have to Him. Confess how little you understand what God is willing to do for you, and say each time as you pray, "And now, Lord, what wait I for?" My heart cannot say. God's heart knows and waits to give. "My hope is in thee." Wait on God to do for you more than you can ask or think.

Apply this to the prayer that follows: "Deliver me from all my transgressions." You have prayed to be delivered from temper, or pride, or self-will. It is as if it is in vain. Could it be that you have had your own thoughts about the way or the extent of God's doing it, and have never waited on the God of glory, according to the riches of His glory, to do for you what has not entered the heart of man to imagine? Learn to worship God as the God who does wonders, who wishes to prove in you that He can do something supernatural and divine. Bow before Him, wait on Him, until your soul realizes that you are in the hands of a divine and almighty worker. Consent to know only what and how He will work. Expect it to be something altogether godlike, something to be waited for in deep humility, and received only by His divine power. Let the "And now, Lord, what wait I for? my hope is in thee" become the spirit of every longing and every prayer. He will in His time do His work.

Believer, in waiting on God you may often be weary, because you hardly know what to expect. But I beg you, be of good courage—this ignorance is often one of the best signs. He is teaching you to leave everything in His hands, and to wait on Him alone. "Wait on the Lord! Be strong, and let your heart take courage. Yea, wait thou on the Lord."

My soul, wait only on God!

14

The Way to the New Song

"I waited patiently for the Lord; and he inclined unto me, and heard my cry. . . . And he hath put a new song in my mouth, even praise unto our God" (Ps. 40:1, 3).

Come and listen to the testimony of one who can speak from experience of the sure and blessed outcome of patient waiting on God. True patience is so foreign to our self-confident nature, yet so indispensable in our waiting on God. It is such an essential element of true faith that we will once again meditate on what the Word has to teach us.

The word patience is derived from the Latin word for suffering. It suggests the thought of being under the constraint of some power from which we are eager to be free. At first we submit against our will. Experience teaches us that when it is useless to resist, patient endurance is our wisest alternative. In waiting on God it is important that we submit not because we are forced to, but because we lovingly and joyfully consent to be in the hands of our blessed Father. Patience then becomes our highest blessing and our highest grace. It honors God and gives Him time to have His way with us. It is the highest expression of our faith in His goodness and faithfulness. It brings the soul perfect rest in the assurance that God is carrying on His work. It is the evidence of our full consent that God should deal with us in a way and time that He thinks best. True patience is the losing of our self-will in His perfect will.

Such patience is needed for true and full waiting on God. Such patience is the growth and fruit of our first lessons in the school of waiting. To many it will appear strange how difficult it is to truly wait on God. The great stillness of soul before God that sinks into its own helplessness and waits for Him to reveal himself; the deep humility that is afraid to let one's own will or own strength work to any degree except as God works to will and to do; the gentleness that is content to be and to know nothing except as God gives His light; the entire resignation of the will that only wants to be a vessel in which His holy will can be revealed and accomplished—all these elements of perfect patience are not found at once. But they will come steadily as the soul maintains its position and says again and again, "Truly my soul waiteth upon God; from him cometh my salvation: he only is my rock and my salvation."

Have you ever noticed what proof we have that patience is a grace for which very *special* grace is given? Paul says to the Colossians: *"Strengthened with all might, according to his glorious power, unto all"*—what? *"Patience and long-suffering with joyfulness."* Yes, we need to be strengthened with all God's might, strengthened as far as His glorious power reaches, if we are to wait on God in *all* patience. It is God revealing himself in us as our life and strength that will enable us with perfect patience to leave everything in His hands. If anyone is inclined to lose hope, because he does not have such patience, be encouraged. It is in the process of our weak and very imperfect waiting that God himself by His hidden power strengthens us and works out in us the patience of the saints, the patience of Christ himself.

Listen to the voice of one who was deeply tried: "I waited patiently for the Lord; and he inclined unto me, and heard my cry." Hear what he passed through: "He brought me up also out of an horrible pit, out of the miry clay, and set my feet upon a rock, and established my goings. And he hath put a new song in my mouth, even praise unto our God." Patient waiting on God brings a rich reward; the deliverance is sure; God himself will put a new song in your mouth. O believer, do not be impatient, whether it is in the exercise of prayer and worship that you find difficulty in waiting, or in persisting for an answer to prayer, or in the fulfilling of your heart's desire for the revelation of God himself in a deeper spiritual life! Don't be discouraged, but rest in the Lord, and wait patiently for Him. And if you sometimes feel as if patience is not your gift, then remember *it is* God's gift, and take that prayer from 2 Thessalonians 3:5: "The Lord direct your hearts into the . . . patience of Christ." Into the patience with which you are to wait on God, He himself will guide you.

My soul, wait only on God!

15

For His Counsel

"They soon forgat his works; they waited not for his counsel" (Ps. 106:13).

This is said of the sin of God's people in the wilderness. He had wonderfully redeemed them, and was prepared to just as wonderfully supply all their needs. But, when the time of need came, "they waited not for his counsel." They did not remember that the almighty God was their leader and provider; they did not ask what His plans might be. They simply thought the thoughts of their own hearts, and tempted and provoked God by their unbelief. "They waited not for his counsel."

This has so often been the sin of God's people throughout history! In the land of Canaan, in the days of Joshua, the only three failures of which we read were due to this one sin. In going against Ai, in making a covenant with the Gibeonites, in settling down without going up to possess the whole land, they did not wait for His counsel. And so even the advanced believer is in danger of this most subtle temptation—taking God's Word and thinking his own thoughts about it, and not waiting for His counsel. Let us take the warning and see what Israel teaches us. And let us especially regard it not only as a danger to which the individual is exposed, but as one against which God's people collectively need to be on their guard.

Our whole relationship to God is found in this, that His will is to be done in us and by us as it is in heaven. He has promised to make known His will to us by His Spirit, our guide into all truth. And our position is to be that of waiting for His counsel as the only guide of our thoughts and actions. In our church worship, in our prayer meetings, in our conventions, in all our gatherings as managers, or directors, or committees, or helpers in any part of the work for God, our first object should always be to find out what is on God's mind. God always works according to the counsel of His will. The more that counsel of His will is looked for and found and honored, the more surely and mightily will God do His work for us and through us.

The great danger in all these type of meetings is that in our consciousness of having our Bible, and our past experience of God's leading, and our accurate creed, and our honest wish to do God's will, we trust in these, and do not realize that with every step we need and may have a heavenly guidance. There may be elements of God's will, application of His Word, experience of His close presence and leading, and a manifestation of the power of His Spirit about which we know nothing at this time. God may be willing, no, God *is* willing to open these up to the souls who are intently set on allowing Him to have His way entirely, and who are willing in patience to wait for Him to make it known. When we come together praising God for all He has done and taught and given, we may at the same time be limiting Him by not expecting greater things. It was when God had given the water out of the rock that they did not trust Him for bread. It was when God had given Jericho into his hands that Joshua thought the victory over Ai was sure, and did not wait for counsel from God. And so, while we think we know and trust the power of God for what we may expect, we may be hindering Him by not giving time, and not definitely practicing the habit of waiting for His counsel.

A minister has no duty more serious than teaching people to wait on God. Why was it that in the house of Cornelius, when "Peter spake these words, the Holy Ghost fell upon all that heard him"? They had said, "We are here *before* God to hear all things that are commanded thee *of God*." We may come together to give and to listen to the most fervent exposition of God's truth with little or no spiritual profit if there is no waiting for God's counsel.

And so in all our gatherings we need to believe in the Holy Spirit as the guide and teacher of God's saints when they wait to be led by Him into the things which God has prepared, and of which the heart cannot conceive.

More stillness of soul to realize God's presence; more consciousness of ignorance of what God's great plans may be; more faith in the certainty that God has greater things to show us, that He himself will be revealed in new glory—these must be the marks of the meetings of God's saints if they want to avoid this disgrace: "They waited not for his counsel."

My soul, wait only on God!

16

And His Light in the Heart

"I wait for the Lord, my soul doth wait, and in his word do I hope. My soul waiteth for the Lord more than they that watch for the morning: I say, more than they that watch for the morning" (Ps. 130:5, 6).

The morning light is often waited for with intense longing. By the sailors in a shipwrecked vessel; by a nighttime traveler in a dangerous country; by an army that finds itself surrounded by an enemy. The morning light will show what hope of escape there may be. The morning may bring life and liberty. In the same way, the saints of God, living in darkness of this world, have longed for the light of His countenance more than watchmen for the morning. They have said, more than watchmen for the morning, my soul waits for the Lord. Can we say that too? Our waiting on God can have no higher goal than simply having His light shine on us, and in us, and through us, all day long.

God is light. God is like a sun. Paul says, "God hath shined in our hearts to give the light." What light? "The light of the glory of God, in the face of Jesus Christ." Just as the sun shines its beautiful, life-giving light on and into our earth, so God shines in our hearts the light of His glory, of His love, in Christ His Son. Our heart is meant to have that light filling and brightening it all day long. It can have it because God is our sun, and it is written, "Thy sun shall no more go down forever." God's love shines on us without ceasing.

But can we indeed enjoy it all day long? We can. And how can we? Let nature give us the answer. Those beautiful trees and flowers, with all the green grass, what do they do to keep the sun shining on them? They do nothing; they simply relax in the sunshine, when it comes. The sun is millions of miles away, but over all that distance it comes, its own light and joy; and the tiniest flower that lifts its little head upward is met by the same radiance of light and blessing that illuminates the widest landscape. We do not have to worry about the light we need for our day's work. The sun cares and provides and shines the light around us all day long. We simply count on it, and receive it, and enjoy it.

The only difference between nature's light and God's light is this, what the trees and the flowers do unconsciously, as they drink in the blessing of the light, we are to do with a voluntary and a loving acceptance. Faith, simple faith in God's Word and love, is to be the thing that opens the eyes and opens the heart, to receive and enjoy the indescribable glory of His grace. And just as the trees, day by day, and month by month, stand and grow into beauty and fruitfulness, welcoming whatever sunshine the sun may give, so it is the very highest exercise of our Christian life to abide in the light of God, and let it, and let Him, fill us with the life and the brightness it brings.

And if you ask, Can it really be, that just as naturally and heartily as I recognize and rejoice in the beauty of a bright sunny morning, I can rejoice in God's light all day long? Yes, you really can. From my breakfast table I look out on a beautiful valley, with trees and vineyards and mountains. In our spring and autumn months the light in the morning is incomparable, and impulsively we say, How beautiful! The questions still come, Is it only the light of the sun that is to bring such continual beauty and joy? Is there no way for the light of God to be just as much a continual source of joy and gladness? There certainly is, if the soul will simply be still and wait on Him, *only let God shine.*

Believer, learn to wait on the Lord, more than those who watch for the morning! Inside you may be very dark. But that is the very best reason for waiting for the light of God. The first beginnings of light may be just enough to discover the darkness, and painfully to humble you on account of sin. Can you not trust the light to expel the darkness? Believe that it will. Simply bow, even now, in stillness before God and wait on Him to shine in you. Say, in humble faith, God is light, infinitely brighter and more beautiful than the light of the sun. God the Father is light. The Son is eternal, inaccessible, and incomprehensible light. The Spirit is light concentrated and manifested—the light entering and dwelling and shining in our hearts. God is light and is shining in my heart. I have been so occupied with the searchlights of my thoughts and efforts, I have never opened the shutters to let His light in. Unbelief has kept it out. I bow in faith—God, light, is shining into my heart. The God of whom Paul wrote, "God hath shined into our heart," is my God. What would I think of a sun that could not shine? What will I think of a God who does not shine? No, God shines! God is light! I will take time, and simply be still, and rest in the light of God. My eyes are weak, and the windows are not clean, but I will wait on the Lord. The light does shine, the light will shine in me, and make me full of light. And I shall learn to walk all day long in the light and joy of God. My soul waits on the Lord, more than the watchers for the morning.

My soul, wait only on God!

17

In Times of Darkness

"I will wait upon the Lord, that hideth his face from the house of Jacob, and I will look for him" (Isa. 8:17).

Here we have a servant of God, waiting on Him, not for himself, but for his people, from whom God was hiding His face. It suggests to us how our waiting on God, though it begins with our personal needs, with the desire for the revelation of himself, or for the answer to personal requests, it does not need to stop there. We may be walking in the full light of God's approval while God is hiding His face from His people around us. Far from being content to think that this is the punishment they deserve for their sin, or the consequence of their indifference, we are called with tender hearts to think of their sad condition, and to wait on God in their behalf. The privilege of waiting on God is one that brings great responsibility. Christ entered God's presence and at once used His position of privilege and honor as intercessor. With the same determination, if we know what it is to enter in and wait on God, we must use our access for those who still live in darkness. "I will wait upon the Lord, who hideth his face from the house of Jacob."

You worship with a certain congregation. Perhaps you do not find the spiritual life or joy either in the preaching or in the fellowship that you desire. Perhaps there is so much error or worldliness, or seeking after human wisdom and culture, or trust in formalities and observances, that you can easily see why God hides His face and why there is so little power for conversion or true edification. Then there are branches of Christian work with which you are connected—a Sunday school, an outreach committee, a men's prayer breakfast, a mission work abroad—in which the absence of the Spirit's working appears to indicate that God is hiding His face. You think you know the reason here, too. There is too much trust in men and money; too much formality and self-indulgence; too little faith and prayer; too little love and humility; too little of the spirit of the crucified Jesus. At times you feel as if things are hopeless; nothing will help.

Believe that God can and will help. Let the spirit of the prophet come into you, as you meditate on his words, and set yourself to wait on God, on behalf of His people who have gone astray. Instead of feeling judgment, condemnation, or despair, realize your calling to wait on God. If others fail in doing it, give yourself to it twice as much. The deeper the darkness, the greater the need of appealing to the one and only deliverer. The more you see self-confidence in people around you, not knowing they are poor and miserable and blind, the more urgent the call is to *you* who profess to see the evil and have access to Him who alone can help, to be on your knees waiting on God. Each time you are tempted to criticize or shake your head, say instead: "I will wait on the Lord, who hideth his face from the house of Jacob."

There is a larger circle yet—the Christian church throughout the world. Think of Greek Orthodox, Roman Catholic, and Protestant churches, and the condition of the millions that belong to them. Or think of only the Protestant churches with all their Bibles and orthodox creeds. There is so much easy believism and tradition! So much rule of the flesh and of man in the very temple of God! This is such a convincing proof that God does hide His face!

What are those who see this and are grieved to do? The first thing to do is hear the psalmist: "I will wait on the Lord, who hideth his face from the house of Jacob." We must wait on God, making humble confession of the sins of His people. We need to take time and wait on Him. Let us wait on God in tender, loving intercession for all believers, however wrong their lives or their teaching may appear. Wait on God in faith and expectation until He shows you that He hears. Let us wait on God, with the simple offering of ourselves and with the sincere prayer that He will draw all men to himself. Let us wait on God and give Him no rest till He makes Zion a joy in the earth. Yes, rest in the Lord and wait patiently for Him who now hides His face from so many of His children. And let us say this about the approval of God that we long to see for all His people, "I wait for the Lord, my soul doth wait, and in his word do I hope. My soul waiteth for the Lord, more than they that watch for the morning: I say, more than they that watch for the morning."

My soul, wait only on God!

18

To Reveal Himself

"And it shall be said in that day, Lo, this is our God; we have waited for him, and he will save us: this is the Lord; we have waited for him, we will be glad and rejoice in his salvation" (Isa. 25:9).

In this passage we have two important thoughts. First, we see that the language indicates God's people have been waiting on Him together. The second is that the result of their waiting has been that God has so revealed himself that they could joyfully say, "Lo, this is our God . . . this is the Lord." The power and the blessing of waiting together is what we need to learn.

Note the twice-repeated phrase: "We have waited for him." In a time of trouble the hearts of the people had been drawn together, and they had, giving up all human hope or help, with one heart set themselves to wait for their God. Is not this just what we need in our churches, conventions, and prayer meetings? The need of the church and the world demands it. There are evils in the church of Christ to which no human wisdom is equal: ritualism, rationalism, formalism and worldliness—all robbing the church of its power. Then, too,

83

there is culture, money and pleasure that threaten its spiritual life. It seems that the powers of the church are so inadequate to cope with the power of unfaithfulness, disobedience, and misery both in so-called Christian countries and in those where the gospel is not known. And yet, is there not in the promises of God and in the power of the Holy Spirit a provision made to meet these needs, and give the church the restful assurance that she is doing all her God expects of her? Would not waiting on God for the supply of His Spirit most certainly bring the needed blessing? There is no doubt it would.

The *purpose* of a more definite waiting on God in our gatherings would be very much the same as in personal worship. It would mean a deeper conviction that God must and will do all; a more humble and constant awareness of our deep helplessness, and the need of entire dependence on Him; a more vivid consciousness that the essential thing is to give God His place of honor and of power; a confident expectation that to those who wait on Him, God will, by His Spirit, give the secret of His acceptance and presence, and then, in due time, the revelation of His saving power. The *purpose* would be to bring everyone in a praying and worshiping congregation to a deeper sense of God's presence, so that when they part there will be the consciousness of having met God himself, of having left every request with Him, and of now waiting in stillness while He works out His salvation.

It is this experience that is indicated in our text. The comparable experience in a modern setting may, at times, come with such astounding interventions of God's power that all can join in the cry: "Lo, this is our God . . . this is the Lord!" It may equally come in spiritual experience, when God's people in their waiting times become so conscious of His presence that in holy awe souls feel: "Lo, this is our God . . . this is the Lord!" It is this experience, sadly enough, that is too often missing in our meetings for worship. The godly minister has no more difficult, no more solemn, no more blessed task, than to lead his people out to meet God, and, before he preaches, to bring each one into contact with Him. "We are now here in the presence of God"— these words of Cornelius show the way in which Peter's audience was prepared for the coming of the Holy Spirit. Waiting before God, waiting for God, and waiting on God, make up the one condition of God showing His presence.

A congregation of believers gathered with this one purpose, helping each other by short intervals of silence, to wait on God alone, opening the heart for whatever God may have of new discoveries of evil, of His will, of new openings in work or methods of work, would soon have reason to say: "Lo, this is our God; we have waited for him, and he will save us: this is the Lord; we have waited for him, we will be glad and rejoice in his salvation."

My soul, wait only on God!

19

As a God of Judgment

"Yea, in the way of thy judgments, O Lord, have we waited for thee . . . for when thy judgments are in the earth, the inhabitants of the world will learn righteousness" (Isa. 26:8, 9).

"The Lord is a God of judgment: blessed are all they that wait for him" (Isa. 30:18).

God is a God of mercy and a God of judgment. Mercy and judgment are always together in His dealings. In the Flood, in the deliverance of Israel out of Egypt, in the overthrow of the Canaanites, we constantly see mercy in the midst of judgment. In the inner circle of His own people we see it too. The judgment punishes the sin, while mercy saves the sinner. Or rather, mercy saves the sinner, not in spite of, but by means of, the very judgment that came on his sin. In waiting on God, we must beware of forgetting this—as we wait we must expect Him as a God of judgment.

"In the way of thy judgments, O Lord, have we waited for thee." That will prove true in our inner experience. If we are honest in our longing for holiness, in our prayer to be wholly the Lord's, His holy presence will stir up and discover hidden sin, and bring us very low in the bitter conviction of the evil of our nature, its opposition to God's law, its resistance to fulfill that law. The words will come true: "Who may abide the day of his coming, for he is like a refiner's fire." "O that thou wouldest come down, as when the melting fire burneth!" In great mercy God executes, within the soul, His judgments on sin, as He makes it feel its wickedness and guilt. Many try to flee from these judgments. The soul that longs for God, and for deliverance from sin, bows under them in humility and in hope. In silence of soul it says, "Arise, O Lord! and let thine enemies be scattered. In the way of thy judgments we have waited for thee."

No one who seeks to learn the blessed art of waiting on God should be surprised if at first the attempt to wait on Him only discovers more of his sin and darkness. Let no one despair because unconquered sins, evil thoughts, or great darkness appear to hide God's face. After all, in His own beloved Son, the gift and bearer of His mercy on Calvary, mercy was in the same way hidden and lost in that judgment. Oh, submit and sink down deep under the judgment of your every sin. Judgment prepares the way and breaks out in wonderful mercy. It is written: "Thou shalt be redeemed with judgment." Wait on God, in the faith that His tender mercy is working out His redemption in the midst of judgment. Wait for Him. He will be gracious to you.

There is one more application, one of indescribable seriousness. We are expecting God, *in the way of His judgments*, to visit this earth: we are waiting for Him. What a thought! We know of these coming judgments; we know that there are tens of thousands of professing Christians who live on in carelessness, and who, if no change is made, must perish under God's hand. Oh, will we not do our utmost to warn them, to plead with and for them, that perhaps God may have mercy on them! If we feel our want of boldness, want of zeal, want of power, should we not begin to wait on God more definitely and persistently as a God of judgment, asking Him to so reveal himself in the judgments that are coming on our friends that we may be inspired with a new fear of Him and His judgments, and sense the urgency to speak and pray as never before? It is true, waiting on God is not meant to be a spiritual self-indulgence. Its object is to let God and His holiness, Christ and the love that died on Calvary, the Spirit and fire that burns in heaven and came to earth, get possession of us, to warn and stir up men with the message that we are waiting for God in the way of His judgments. Oh, Christian, prove that you really believe in the God of judgment!

My soul, wait only on God!

20

Who Waits on Us

"And therefore will the Lord wait, that he may be gracious unto you, and therefore will he be exalted, that he may have mercy upon you: for the Lord is a God of judgment: blessed are all they that wait for him" (Isa. 30:18).

We must not only think of our waiting on God, but also of what is more wonderful than that: God's waiting on us. The vision of Him waiting on us will give new impulse and inspiration to our waiting on Him. It will give an indescribable confidence that our waiting cannot be in vain. If He waits for us, then we may be sure that we are more than welcome, that He rejoices to find those for whom He has been seeking. Let us seek even now, at this moment, in the spirit of humble waiting on God, to find out something of what it means: "Therefore will the Lord wait, that he may be gracious unto you." We will accept and echo back the message: "Blessed *are all they* that wait for him."

Look up and see the great God on His throne. He is Love—a continuous and inexpressible desire to communicate His own goodness and blessedness to all His creatures. He longs and delights to bless. He has inconceivably glorious plans concerning every one of His children, by the power of His Holy Spirit, to reveal in them His love and power. He waits with all the anticipation of a father's heart. He waits so that He may be gracious to you. And each time you come to wait on Him, or seek to maintain in daily life the holy habit of waiting, you may look up and see Him ready to meet you, waiting so that He may be gracious to you. Yes, connect every activity, every breath of the life of waiting, with faith's vision of your God waiting for you.

And if you ask, How is it, if He waits to be gracious, that even after I come and wait on Him, He does not give the help I seek, but waits on longer and longer? There is a twofold answer. The *first* is this. God is a farmer, "who waiteth for the precious fruit of the earth, and hath long patience for it." He cannot gather the crop till it is ripe. He knows when we are spiritually ready to receive the blessing to our profit and His glory. Waiting in the sunshine of His love is what will ripen the soul for His blessing. Waiting under the cloud of trial, that breaks in showers of blessing, is essential. Be assured that if God waits longer than you wish, it is only to make the blessing all the more precious. God waited four thousand years, till the fullness of time, before He sent His Son. Our times are in His hands. He will see that justice is done for His chosen people speedily. He is in a hurry to help us, and will not delay one hour too long.

The *second* answer points to what has been said before. The giver is more than the gift; God is more than the blessing; and our time spent waiting on Him is the only way for us to learn to find our life and joy *in Him*. Oh, if God's children only knew what a glorious God they have, and what a privilege it is to be linked in fellowship with Him. Then they would rejoice in Him! Even when He keeps them waiting, they would learn to understand better than ever: "Therefore will the Lord wait, that he may be gracious unto you." His waiting will be the highest proof of His graciousness.

"Blessed are all they that wait for him." A queen has her ladies-in-waiting. The position is one of subordination and service, and yet it is considered to be a position of the highest dignity and privilege, because a wise and gracious ruler makes them companions and friends. What an honor and blessing to be attendants-in-waiting on the everlasting God, always on the watch for every indication of His will or favor, always conscious of His nearness, His goodness, and His grace! "The Lord is good to them that wait for him." "Blessed are all they that wait for him." Yes, it is a blessing when a waiting soul and a waiting God meet each other. God cannot do His work without His and our waiting for His time. Let waiting be our work, as it is His. And if His waiting is nothing but goodness and graciousness, let ours be nothing but a rejoicing in that goodness and a confident expectancy of that grace. And let every thought of waiting become to us simply the expression of pure blessing, because it brings us to a God who waits so that He may make himself known to us perfectly as the gracious One.

My soul, wait only on God!

21

The Almighty One

"They that wait upon the Lord shall renew their strength; they shall mount up with wings as eagles; they shall run, and not be weary; and they shall walk, and not faint" (Isa. 40:31).

Waiting is always affected by what exists in our thoughts about the one on whom we wait. Our waiting on God will depend greatly on our faith in what He is. In our text we have the close of a passage in which God reveals himself as the everlasting and almighty One. It is as that revelation enters our soul that the waiting will become the spontaneous expression of what we know Him to be—a God altogether most worthy of being waited on.

Listen to the words: "Why sayest thou, Jacob, my way is hid from the Lord?" Why do you speak as if God does not hear or help?

"Hast thou not known, hast thou not heard, that the everlasting One, the Lord, the creator of the ends of the earth, *fainteth not, neither is weary*? Far from it: "He giveth power to the faint, and to them that have no might he increaseth strength. Even the youths"—"the glory of young men is their strength"—"even the youths shall faint, and the young men shall utterly fall." All that is considered to be strong with man will come to nothing. "*But* they that wait on the Lord," on the everlasting One, who does not faint and does not get weary, they "shall renew their strength; they shall mount up with wings as eagles; they shall run, and"—listen now—they shall be strong with the strength of God in the same way as He *will* "*not be weary*; and they shall walk, and," like Him, "*not faint.*"

Yes, "they shall mount up with wings as eagles." You know what eagles' wings mean. The eagle is the king of birds and soars the highest into the skies. Believers are to live a heavenly life, in the actual presence and love and joy of God. They are to live where God lives; they need God's strength, though, to rise there. To those who wait on Him, it will be given.

You know how the eagles' wings are obtained. Only in one way—by the eagles' birth. You are born of God. You *have* the eagles' wings. You may not have known it; you may not have used them; but God can and will teach you to use them.

You know how the eagles are taught the use of their wings. Imagine a cliff rising a thousand feet out of the sea. Then see a ledge high up on the rock where there is an eagle's nest with its treasure of two young eaglets. Next, the mother bird comes and stirs up her nest, and with her beak pushes the timid birds over the edge. See how they flutter and fall and sink toward the depth. Now watch as she "fluttereth over her young, spreadeth abroad her wings, taketh them, beareth them on her wings" (Deut. 32:11). And so, as they ride on her wings, she brings them to a place of safety. Then, she does it once and again, each time pushing them out over the edge, and then again taking and carrying them. "So the Lord alone did lead him." Yes, the instinct of that eagle mother was God's gift, a single ray of that love in which the almighty trains His people to mount as on eagles' wings.

He stirs up your nest. He prolongs your hopes. He tries your confidence. He makes you fear and tremble, as all your strength fails, and you feel utterly weary and helpless. And all the while He is spreading His strong wings for you to rest your weakness on, and offering His everlasting strength to work in you. And all He asks is that you sink down in your weariness and *wait on Him*; and allow Him in His Jehovah-strength to carry as you ride on the wings of His omnipotence.

Dear believer, I beg you, lift up your eyes and *behold your God!* Listen to Him who says that He "fainteth not, neither is weary," who promises that you too will not faint or be weary, who asks nothing but this one thing, that you should *wait on Him*. And let your answer be, With such a God, so mighty, so faithful, so tender, I will wait on Him.

My soul, wait only on God!

22

Its Certainty of Blessing

"Thou shalt know that I am the Lord: for they shall not be ashamed that wait for me" (Isa. 49:23).
"Blessed are all they that wait for him" (Isa. 30:18).

What promises! God tries to get us to wait on Him by the most positive assurance. He says it can *never* be in vain: "They shall not be ashamed that wait for me." It is so strange that, though we should so often have experienced it, we are still very slow to learn that this waiting must and can be the very breath of our life, a continuous resting in God's presence and His love, a constant yielding of ourselves for Him to perfect His work in us. Let us once again listen and meditate until our heart says with new conviction: *"Blessed are they* that wait for him!" In chapter six we found in the prayer of Psalm 25: "Let none that wait on thee be ashamed." The fact that the prayer exists at all shows how we fear that some might be disappointed. Let us listen to God's answer until every fear is driven away and we send back to heaven the words God speaks. Lord, we believe what you say: *"All they* that wait for me shall *not* be ashamed." "Blessed are *all they* that wait for him."

The context of each of these two passages points us to times when God's church was in a very difficult situation, and to the human eye there were no possibilities of deliverance. But God intervenes with His word of promise, and pledges His almighty power for the deliverance of His people. And it is God himself who has undertaken the work of their redemption and invites them to wait on him, assuring them that disappointment is impossible. We too are living in days in which there is so much in the condition of the church, with its hypocrisy and its traditionalism, that is indescribably sad. Even with all we have to praise God for, there is, unfortunately, much to mourn over! If it were not for God's promises, we would have good reason to despair. But in His promises the living God has given, and bound himself to us. He calls us to wait on Him. He assures us that we will not be put to shame. If our hearts could only learn to wait before Him until He himself reveals to us what His promises mean, and in the promises reveals himself in His hidden glory, we would then be powerfully drawn to wait on Him alone. May God increase the number of those who say: "Our soul waiteth for the Lord: he is our help and our shield."

This waiting on God on behalf of His church and people will depend greatly on the place that waiting on Him has taken in our personal life. Our minds may often have beautiful visions of what God has promised to do, and our lips may speak of them in exciting words, but these are not really the measure of our faith or power. No; it is what we really know of God in our personal experience, conquering the enemies within, reigning and ruling, revealing himself in His holiness and power in our inmost being. It is this revealing that will be the true measure of the spiritual blessing we expect from Him, and bring to our fellowmen. It is as we know how waiting on God has become a blessing to our own souls that we will confidently hope for the blessing to come on the church around us, and the theme of all our expectations will be, He has said: "All they that wait on me shall not be ashamed." From what He has done in us, we will trust Him to do mighty things around us. "Blessed are all they that wait for him." Yes, blessed even now in the waiting. The promised blessings for ourselves, or for others, may be delayed. But the immeasurable blessing of knowing and having Him who has promised, the living fountain of the coming blessings, is already ours. Be sure to let this truth get full possession of your souls, that waiting on God is itself the highest privilege of the creature, the highest blessing for His redeemed child.

In the same way that the sunshine enters with its light and warmth, with its beauty and blessing, into every little blade of grass that rises upward out of the cold earth, so the everlasting God meets, in the greatness and the tenderness of His love, each waiting child, to shine in his heart "the light of the knowledge of the glory of God in the face of Jesus Christ." Read these words again until your heart learns to know what God waits to do to you. Who can measure the difference between the great sun and that little blade of grass? And yet the grass has all of the sun it needs or can hold. Believe that in waiting on God, His greatness and your littleness suit and meet each other most wonderfully. Just bow in emptiness and poverty, in complete powerlessness and humility, and surrender to His will before His great glory, and be still. As you wait on Him, God comes near. He will reveal himself as the God who will fulfill mightily every one of His promises. And let your heart continue to repeat this promise: "Blessed are all they that wait for him."

My soul, wait only on God!

23

For Inconceivable Things

"For since the beginning of the world men have not heard, nor perceived by the ear, neither hath the eye seen, O God, beside thee, what he hath prepared for him that waiteth for him" (Isa. 64:4).

The American Standard Version has: *"Neither hath the eye seen a God besides thee, who worketh for him that waiteth for him."* In the King James Version the thought is, that no eye has seen *the thing* which God has prepared. In the ASV no eye has seen a *God*, besides our God, who works for him that waits for Him. In both versions the two other thoughts are the same: that our responsibility is to wait on God, and that there will be revealed to us what the human heart cannot conceive. The only difference is: in the ASV it is *the God* who works, and in the KJV it is *the thing* He is to work. In 1 Corinthians 2:9, the quotation of this verse is in regard to the things which the Holy Spirit is to reveal, as the KJV passage from Isaiah indicates. In this meditation we will keep to that interpretation.

The previous verses, especially from chapter 63:15, refer to the low state of God's people. The prayer has been poured out, "Look down from heaven" (v. 15). "Why hast thou . . . hardened our heart from thy fear? Return for thy servants' sake" (v. 17). And 64:1, still more urgent, "Oh that thou wouldest rend the heavens, that thou wouldest come down . . . as when the melting fire burneth . . . to make thy name known to thy adversaries!" Then follows the plea from the past: "When thou didst terrible things which we looked not for, thou camest down, the mountains flowed down at thy presence." "For"—now we will see the faith that has been awakened by the thought of things that had not been looked for, He is still the same God—"neither hath the eye seen, O God, beside thee, what he hath prepared for him that waiteth for him." God alone knows what He can do for His waiting people. As Paul explains and applies it: "The things of God knoweth no man, save the Spirit of God." "But God hath revealed them to us by his Spirit."

The need of God's people, and the call for God's intervention, is as urgent in our days as it was in the time of Isaiah. There is now, as there was then, as there has been at all times, a remnant that seek after God with their whole heart. But if we look at all Christians as a whole, at the condition of the church of Christ, there is infinite reason to ask God to rend the heavens and come down. Nothing but a special intervention of almighty power will accomplish what is needed. I fear that we do not have a right conception of what the so-called Christian world is in the sight of God. Unless God comes down "as when the melting fire burneth . . . to make known his name to his adversaries," our labors are comparatively fruitless. Look at the ministry. So much of it is in the wisdom of man and of literary academics. So little is in demonstration of the Spirit and of power. Think of the unity of the body—how little there is of the manifestation of the power of a heavenly love binding God's children into one. Think of holiness—by that I mean the holiness of Christlike humility and crucifixion to the world—how little the world sees that they have men among them who live in Christ in heaven, and in whom Christ lives.

What is to be done? There is only one thing. We must wait on God. And what for? We must cry, with a cry that never rests, "Oh that thou wouldest rend the heavens . . . come down, that the mountains might flow down at thy presence!" We must desire and believe, we must ask and expect, that God will do inconceivable things. We must set our faith on a God of whom men do not know what He has prepared for them that wait for Him. The miracle-working God, who can surpass all our expectations, must be the God of our confidence.

Yes, let God's people enlarge their hearts to wait on a God able to do much, much more than what we can ask or think. Let us band ourselves together as His chosen people who cry day and night to Him for things men have not seen. He is able to come and to make His people a name and a praise in the earth. "He will wait, that he may be gracious unto you; blessed are all they that wait for him."

My soul, wait only on God!

24

To Know His Goodness

"The Lord is good unto them that wait for him" (Lam. 3:25).

"There is none good but God." "His goodness is in the heavens." "Oh how great is thy goodness, which thou hast laid up for them that fear thee!" "O taste and see that the Lord is good!" The *way* of entering into and rejoicing in this goodness of God is made clear in this verse—waiting on Him. The Lord is good. His own children often do not know it, for they do not wait in quietness for Him to reveal it. But to those who persevere in waiting, whose souls do wait, it will come true. You might think that it is just those who have to wait who might doubt it. But this is only when they do *not* wait, but grow impatient. The truly waiting ones will all have to say: "The Lord is good unto them that wait for him." Do you want to fully know the goodness of God? Give yourself more than ever to a life of waiting on Him.

As we first enter the school of waiting on God, our hearts are chiefly set on the blessings we wait for. God graciously uses our need and desire for help to educate us for something higher than we were thinking of. We were seeking gifts; He, the giver, longs to give himself and to satisfy the soul with His goodness. It is exactly for this reason that He often withholds the gifts, and that the time of waiting is made so long. He is all the time seeking to win the heart of His child for himself. He hopes that we will not only say, when He gives the gift, How good is God! but that long before it comes, and even if it never comes, we will always be experiencing: *It is good* that a man should quietly wait: "The Lord *is good* to them that wait for him."

What a blessed life the life of waiting then becomes—the continual worship of faith, adoring and trusting His goodness. As your soul learns this secret, every act or exercise of waiting simply becomes a quiet entering into the goodness of God, to let it do its blessed work and satisfy all our needs. And every experience of God's goodness gives the work of waiting new attractiveness. Instead of taking refuge only in time of need, there comes a great longing to wait continually and all day long. And however our duties and daily responsibilities occupy our time and minds, our souls get more familiar with the secret art of always waiting. Waiting becomes the habit and constant attitude, the second nature and breath of your soul.

Dear believer, are you beginning to see that waiting is not one among a number of Christian characteristics to be thought of from time to time, but that it expresses the attitude which lies at the very root of the Christian life? It gives a higher value and a new power to our prayer and worship, to our faith and surrender, because it links us, in inseparable dependence, to God himself. And it gives us the unbroken enjoyment of the goodness of God: "The Lord is good unto them that wait for him."

Let me urge you once again to take time and trouble

to develop this much-needed element of the Christian life. We get too much of *Christianity* secondhand from the teaching of men. That teaching has great value, like John the Baptist's, which directed his disciples away from himself to the living Christ, if it leads us to God himself. What our Christianity needs is *more of God*. Many of us are too occupied with our work. As with Martha, the very service we want to give to the Master separates us from Him. It is neither pleasing to Him nor profitable to ourselves. The more work, the more need of waiting on God. When we believe this truth, the doing of God's will, instead of exhausting us, will be our meat and drink, nourishment and refreshment and strength. "The Lord is good unto them that wait for him." *How* good can be told only by those who prove it in waiting on Him. Only those who have proved Him the most can tell how good He is.

My soul, wait only on God!

25

Quietly

"It is good that a man should both hope and quietly wait for the salvation of the Lord" (Lam. 3:26).

"Take heed, and be *quiet*: fear not, neither be faint-hearted." "In *quietness* and in confidence shall be your strength." Verses like these bring to our attention the close connection between quietness and faith, and show us what a deep need there is for quietness, as an element of true waiting on God. If we are to have our whole heart turned toward God, we must have it turned away from all created things, from all that occupies our time and holds our interest, whether they inspire joy or sorrow.

God is a being of such infinite greatness and glory, and our nature has become so far removed from His, that it takes our whole heart and desire set on Him to in some small way know and receive Him. Everything that is not God, that excites our fears, or stirs our efforts, or awakens our hopes, or makes us glad, stands in the way of our perfect waiting on Him. The message is one with a deep meaning: "Take heed and be quiet";

"In quietness shall be your stength"; "It is good that a man should quietly wait."

The very thought of God in His majesty and holiness should silence us. Over and over the Scriptures tell of this truth.

"The Lord is in his holy temple: let all the earth keep silence before him" (Hab. 2:20).

"Hold thy peace at the presence of the Lord God" (Zeph. 1:7).

"Be silent, O all flesh, before the Lord: for he is raised up out of his holy habitation" (Zech. 2:13).

As long as waiting on God is mainly thought of as a step toward more productive prayer, and the obtaining of our requests, this spirit of perfect quietness will not be obtained. But when it is seen that waiting on God is itself an unsurpassed blessing, one of the highest forms of fellowship with the Holy One, the adoration of Him in His glory will consequently humble the soul into a holy stillness, making the way open for God to speak and reveal himself. Then it becomes a living example of the amazing promise that all selfishness and human pride will be humbled: "The haughtiness of man shall be brought down, and the Lord alone shall be exalted in that day."

Everyone who wants to learn the art of waiting on God should remember this lesson: "Take heed, and be quiet"; "It is good that a man quietly wait." Take time to be away from all friends and all duties, all cares and all joys; time to be still and quiet before God. Take time not ony to acquire stillness from man and the world, but from self and its energy. Let the Word and prayer have very high priority; but remember, even these may get in the way of quiet waiting. The activity of the mind in studying the Word, or putting its thoughts into words for prayer, the activities of the heart, with its desires and hopes and fears, may involve us to the point that we do not come to that *still* waiting on the all-glorious One. Our whole being is not allowed to become prostrate in silence before Him. Though at first it may appear difficult to know how to wait quietly, that is, with the activities of the mind and heart for a time repressed, every effort to do it will be rewarded. We will find that it grows on us, and the short period of silent worship will bring a peace and rest that give a blessing not only in prayer but all day long.

"*It is good* that a man should . . . quietly wait for the salvation of the Lord." Yes, it is good. The quietness is the confession of our inability. It will not be done with all our willing and running, with all our thinking and praying, we must receive it from God. It is the confession of our trust that our God will in His time come to our help—the quiet resting in Him alone. It is the confession of our desire to be only what we are, and to let Him work and reveal himself. Be sure to wait quietly. In the soul waiting daily for God to do His wondrous work, let there be a quiet reverence and a constant guard against too much involvement with the world. Then the whole character of that person will display this message: quietly waiting for the salvation of God.

My soul, wait only on God!

26

In Holy Expectancy

"Therefore will I look unto the Lord; I will wait for the God of my salvation: my God will hear me" (Mic. 7:7).

Have you ever read the little book, *Expectation Corners?* If not, get it. It contains one of the best sermons on the text of this chapter. The sermon tells of a king who prepared a city for some of his poor subjects. Not far from them were large storehouses, where everything they could need was supplied if they sent in their requests. There was just one condition—that they should be on the lookout for the answer, so that when the king's messengers came with the answer to their requests, they would always be found waiting and ready to receive them. The sad story goes on to tell of one desponding subject who never expected to get what he asked because he was too unworthy. One day he was taken to the king's storehouses, and there, to his amazement, he saw, with his address on them, all the packages that had been made up for him and sent. There was the garment of praise, and the oil of joy, and the eyesalve, and so much more. They had been to his door, but found it closed; he was not on the lookout. From that time on he learned the lesson Micah still teaches us today. I will "look to the Lord; I will wait for the God of my salvation; my God will hear me."

We have said more than once: Waiting for the answer to prayer is not the whole process of waiting, but only a part. In this chapter we want to understand the truth that it *is* a part, and a very important one. When we have special requests for which we are waiting on God, our waiting must be very definitely with this confident assurance: "My God will hear me." Holy, joyful expectancy is found in the very essence of true waiting. And this type of expectancy is applied not only to the many varied requests every believer makes but especially to the one great request which ought to be the main thing every heart seeks for itself—that the life of God in the soul may have full control. Expecting that Christ may be fully formed within and that we may be filled to all the fullness of God. This is what God has promised. Yet this is what God's people hardly ever seek, very often because they do not believe it is possible. We ought to seek this and dare to expect it because God is able and waiting to work it in us.

But God himself must work it. And for this to happen, our working must cease. We must see how entirely it must be faith in the operation of God who raised Jesus from the dead—just as much as the resurrection, the perfecting of God's life in our souls, is to be directly His work. And waiting has to become more than ever a lingering before God in stillness of soul, depending on Him who raises the dead, and calls the things that are not as though they were.

Just notice how the threefold use of the name of God in our text points us to himself as the one who alone delivers our expectation. "I [will] look to the Lord; I will wait for the God of my salvation; my God will hear me." Everything that is salvation, everything that is good and holy, must be the direct, personal work of God himself within us. Every moment of a life in the will of God there must be the immediate operation of God. And the one thing I have to do is this: to look to the Lord; to wait for the God of my salvation; to hold on to this confident assurance: "My God will hear me."

God says, "Be still, and know that I am God."

There is no stillness like that of the grave. In the grave of Jesus, in sharing His death—death to self with its own will and wisdom, its own strength and energy—there is rest. As we deny our self, and our soul becomes still to God, God will come and show himself. "Be still, and know"; then you will know "that I am God." There is no stillness like the stillness Jesus gives when He speaks, "Peace, be still." In Christ—in His death, *His life*, and in His completed redemption—the soul may be still, and God will come in, take possession, and do His perfect work.

My soul, wait only on God!

27

For Redemption

"Simeon ... was just and devout, waiting for the consolation of Israel: and the Holy Ghost was upon him. ... Anna, a prophetess ... spake of him to all them that looked for redemption in Jerusalem" (Luke 2:25, 36, 38).

Here we have the marks of a waiting believer. *Just*, righteous in all his conduct; *devout*, devoted to God and always walking in His presence; *waiting for the consolation of Israel*, looking for the fulfillment of God's promises; *and the Holy Ghost was on him*. Through devoted waiting he had been prepared for the blessing. And Simeon was not the only one. Anna spoke to all that looked for redemption in Jerusalem. This was the one mark, in the middle of surrounding formalism and worldliness, of a godly group of men and women in Jerusalem. They were waiting on God; looking for His promised redemption.

And now that the consolation of Israel has come, and the redemption has been accomplished, do we still need to wait? We certainly do. But since we look back to the redemption as having already come, will not our waiting differ greatly from those who looked forward to it as coming? It will, especially in two aspects. We now wait on God in the full power of the redemption; and we wait for its full revelation.

Our waiting is now in the full power of the redemption. Christ said: "In that day ye shall know that ye are *in me*. Abide in me." The New Testament teaches us to present ourselves to God "as indeed dead to sin, and alive to God *in Christ Jesus*," "blessed with all spiritual blessings in heavenly places *in Christ Jesus*." Our waiting on God can now be in the wonderful consciousness, formed and maintained by the Holy Spirit within us, that we are accepted in the beloved, that the love that rests on Him rests on us, that we are living in that love, in the actual presence and sight of God. The old saints took their stand on the Word of God. Waiting and hoping on that Word, we too rest on it—but, oh, with far greater privilege it is to be joined to Christ Jesus! In our waiting on God, let this be our confidence: in Christ we have access to the Father; how sure, therefore, we may be that our waiting cannot be vain.

Our waiting differs too in this, that while they waited for a redemption to come, we see it accomplished, and now wait for its revelation *in us*. Christ not only said, "Abide in me," but also "*I in you*." The New Testament not only speaks of us *in Christ* but of Christ *in us* as the greatest mystery of redeeming love. As we maintain our place in Christ day by day, God waits to reveal Christ in us in such a way that He is formed in us, that His mind and attitude and likeness take on form and substance in us, so that each believer can truthfully say, "Christ liveth in me."

My life in Christ up there in heaven and Christ's life in me down here on earth—these two are the complement of each other. And the more my waiting on

God is marked by the living faith *I in Christ*, the more the heart thirsts for and claims Christ in me. And the waiting on God, which began with special needs and prayer, will increasingly be concentrated, as far as our personal life is concerned, on this one thing: Lord, reveal your redemption fully in me; let Christ live in me.

Our waiting differs from that of the old saints in the place we take and the expectations we hold. But actually it is the same: waiting on God, who alone delivers our expectation.

Learn one lesson from Simeon and Anna. It was utterly impossible for them to do anything toward the great redemption—toward the birth of Christ or His death. *It was God's work. They could do nothing but wait.* Are we as absolutely helpless concerning the revelation of Christ in us? We certainly are. God did not work out the great redemption in Christ as a whole, and leave its application in detail to us.

The thought that this is true lies at the root of all our weakness. The revelation of Christ in every individual believer, step by step and moment by moment, is as much the work of God's almightiness as the birth or resurrection of Christ. Until this truth enters and fills us, and we feel that we are just as dependent on God for each moment of our life in the enjoyment of redemption as they were in their waiting for it, our waiting on God will not bring its full blessing. The sense of complete and absolute helplessness, the confidence that God can and will do all—these must be the marks of our waiting just as it was of theirs. As gloriously as God proved himself to them as the faithful and wonder-working God, He will to us too.

My soul, wait only on God!

28

For the Coming of His Son

"[Be] ye yourselves like unto men that wait for their lord" (Luke 12:36).

"Until the appearing of our Lord Jesus Christ: which in his times shall show, who is the blessed and only Potentate, the King of kings, and Lord of lords" (1 Tim. 6:14, 15).

"Turned to God from idols to serve the living and true God; and to wait for his Son from heaven" (1 Thess. 1:9, 10).

Waiting on God in heaven and waiting for His Son from heaven were both initiated in view of the other and cannot be separated. Waiting on God for His presence and power in daily life will be the only true preparation for waiting for Christ in humility and true holiness. Waiting for Christ's coming from heaven to take us to heaven will give waiting on God its true tone of hopefulness and joy. The Father, who in His own time will reveal His Son from heaven, is the God who, as we wait on Him, prepares us for the revelation of His Son. The present life and the coming glory are inseparably connected in God and in us.

There is sometimes a danger of separating them. It is always easier to be involved with the Christianity of the past or the future than to be faithful in the Christianity of our day. As we think about what God has done in the past, or will do in the future, the claim on our lives of present obligations and submission to His working may be ignored. Waiting on God must always lead to waiting for Christ as the glorious outcome of His work; and waiting for Christ must constantly remind us of the necessity of waiting on God as our only proof that the waiting for Christ is in spirit and in truth. There is such a danger of our being more occupied with the *things* that are coming than *with Him* who is to come. There is such an opportunity in the study of coming events for imagination and reason that nothing but deep, humble waiting on God can save us from mistaking the interest and pleasure of intellectual study for the true love of Him and His appearing. All you who claim to wait for Christ's coming, *be sure you wait on God now*. All you who seek to wait on God to reveal His Son in you now, see to it that you do so as men waiting for the revelation of His Son from heaven. The anticipation of that glorious appearing will strengthen you in waiting on God for what He is to do in you now. The same almighty love that is to reveal that glory is working in you already to fit you for it.

"The blessed hope and appearing of the glory of the great God and our Savior Jesus Christ" (Titus 2:13) is one of the great bonds uniting God's church throughout the ages. "He shall come to be glorified in his saints, and to be marveled at in all them that believe." Then we will all meet, and the unity of the body of Christ will be seen in its divine glory. It will be the meeting place and the satisfaction of God's love: Jesus receiving His people and presenting them to the Father. His people meeting Him and worshiping Him in speechless love; His people meeting each other in the ecstacy of God's own love. Let us wait, long for, and love the appearing of our Lord and heavenly Bridegroom. Tender love to Him and tender love to each other is the true and only bridal spirit.

I have a great fear that this is sometimes forgotten. Some beloved brothers speak about the expectancy of faith being the true sign of the bride. Risking criticism, I express a doubt. An unworthy bride, about to be married to a prince, might be thinking only of the position and the riches she is to receive. In the same way, the expectancy of faith might be very strong, while true love is completely absent. We are not in the bride's place when we are deepest in the study of prophetic subjects but when in humility and love we are clinging to our Lord and His people. Jesus refuses to accept our love except when it is love to His disciples. Waiting for His coming means waiting for the glorious unity of the body that is still coming, while we attempt to maintain that unity in humility and love here on earth. Those who love most are the most ready for His coming. Love to each other is the life and beauty of His bride, the church.

And how is this to be brought about? Beloved child of God, if you want to learn the right way to wait for His Son from heaven, live your life waiting on God in heaven. Remember how Jesus lived always waiting on God. He could do nothing by himself. It was God who perfected His Son through suffering and then exalted Him. It is God alone who can give you the deep spiritual life of one who is really waiting for His Son: wait on God for it. Waiting for Christ himself is so different from waiting for things that may come to pass! The latter any Christian can do; the former, God must work in you every day by His Holy Spirit. Therefore all of you who wait on God, look to Him for grace to wait for His Son from heaven in the Spirit which is from heaven. And you who want to wait for His Son, wait on God continually to reveal Christ in you.

The revelation of Christ in us, which is given to those who wait on God, is the true preparation for the full revelation of Christ in glory.

My soul, wait only on God!

29

For the Promise of the Father

"[He] commanded them that they should not depart from Jerusalem, but wait for the promise of the Father" (Acts 1:4).

When we looked at the saints in Jerusalem at the time of Christ's birth, through Simeon and Anna we saw how, though the redemption they waited for has come, the call to waiting is no less urgent now than it was then. We wait for the full revelation in us of what came to them, but what they could barely comprehend. It is the same with waiting for the promise of the Father. In one sense, the fulfillment can never come again as it came at Pentecost. In another sense, with as deep a reality as with the first disciples, we daily need to wait for the Father to fulfill His promise in us.

The Holy Spirit is not a person distinct from the Father in the way two persons on earth are distinct. The Father and the Spirit are never without or separate from each other. The Father is always in the Spirit; the Spirit works nothing but as the Father works in Him. Each moment the same Spirit that is in us is in God too. He who is most full of the Spirit will be the first to

127

wait on God more earnestly so as to further fulfill His promise and to be mightily strengthened by His Spirit in the inner man. The Spirit in us is not a power at our disposal. Nor is the Spirit an independent power, acting apart from the Father and the Son. The Spirit is *the real living presence and the power of the Father* working in us. It is the one who knows that the Spirit is in him who will wait on the Father for the full revelation and experience of what the Spirit's indwelling is, for His increase and abounding more and more.

You can see this in the apostles. They were filled with the Spirit at Pentecost. Not long after this, having returned from the Council where they had been forbidden to preach, when they prayed once more for boldness to speak in His name—a fresh pouring out of the Holy Spirit was the Father's increased fulfillment of His promise.

At Samaria, by the word and the Spirit, many had been converted, and the whole city filled with joy. Hearing the apostles' prayer, the Father once again fulfilled the promise. He fulfilled it to the waiting group in Cornelius' house. You can see the Spirit *abounding* a fourth time in Acts 13. It was when men, filled with the Spirit, prayed and fasted that the promise of the Father was freshly fulfilled and the leading of the Spirit was given from heaven: "Separate me Barnabas and Saul."

Also, in Ephesians we find Paul praying for those who have been sealed with the Spirit, that God would give them the spirit of illumination. And later on, that He would, according to the riches of His glory, strengthen them with might by the Spirit in their inner man.

The Spirit given at Pentecost was not a project that God failed with in heaven, and sent out of heaven to earth. God does not, He cannot, give away anything in that way. When He gives grace, or strength, or life, He gives it by giving himself to work it—it is all inseparable from himself.* It is all the more true with the Holy Spirit. He is God, present and working in us. The only position in which we can count on that working with continuing power is as we, praising for what we have, constantly wait for the Father's promise to be even more mightily fulfilled.

This gives such new meaning and promise to our life of waiting! It teaches us to always maintain the place where the disciples waited at the footstool of the throne. It reminds us of how helpless they were to meet their enemies or to preach to Christ's enemies until they were given power. We too can only be strong in the life of faith or the work of love when we are in direct communication with God and Christ, and they maintain the life of the Spirit in us. The Spirit's abounding in us assures us that God will, through the glorified Christ, work in us a power that can bring to pass unexpected things, even impossible things. There is nothing the Church will not be able to do when her individual members learn to live their lives waiting on God. There are also impossibilities when together, with all of self and the world denied in favor of love, they unite in agreement, waiting for the promise of the Father, which was once so gloriously fulfilled, but is still unexhausted!

Come and let each of us be still as we meditate on this inconceivably great truth: the Father waits to fill the church with the Holy Spirit. And He is ready to fill *me*, let each believer say.

With this faith let there come over the soul a quiet and holy fear, as it waits in stillness to take it all in.

---

*See the note on William Law on pp. 139–140

And let life increasingly become a deep joy in the hope
of the ever-increasing fulfillment of the Father's promise.

My soul, wait only on God!

30

Continually

"Therefore turn thou to thy God: keep mercy and judgment, and wait on thy God continually" (Hos. 12:6).

Continually is one of the essential elements of biological life. Interrupt it for a single hour in a man, and it is lost; he is dead. Continuity, unbroken and ceaseless, is essential to a healthy Christian life. God wants me to be, and God waits to make me, I want to be, and I wait on Him to make me, every moment, what He expects of me and what is acceptable in His sight. If waiting on God is the essence of true religion, the maintenance of the attitude of entire dependence must be continuous. The command of God, "Wait on thy God continually," must be accepted and obeyed. There may be times of special waiting. But the attitude and habit of every soul must be there unchangeably and uninterrupted.

This waiting continually is definitely a necessity. To those who are content with a nominal Christian life, it appears as a special call, something beyond what is essential to be a good Christian. But all who are praying the prayer, "Lord, make me as holy as a forgiven sinner can be made; keep me as near to you as it is possible for me to be; fill me as full of your love as you are willing to do," feel at once that it is something which must be priority. They feel that there can be no unbroken fellowship with God, no full abiding in Christ, no maintaining of victory over sin and readiness for service, without waiting continually on the Lord.

Waiting continually is a possibility. Many think that with the duties of life it is out of the question. They cannot be always thinking of it. Even when they wish to, they forget.

They do not understand that it is a matter of the heart, and that what the heart is full of, occupies it, even when the thoughts are on other things. A father's heart may be filled continuously with intense love and longing for a sick wife or child at home, even though pressing business requires all his thoughts. When *the heart* has learned how entirely powerless it is for one moment to keep itself or produce any good, when it has learned how surely and absolutely God will keep it, when it has, in despair of itself, accepted God's promise to do for it the impossible, it learns to rest in God, and in the middle of occupations and temptations it can wait continually.

This waiting is a promise. God's commands are enablings; Gospel rules of conduct are all promises, a revelation of what our God will do for us. When first you begin waiting on God, it is with frequent intermission and frequent failure. But remember to believe God is watching over you in love and secretly strengthening you in it. There are times when waiting appears to be simply wasting time, but it is not so. Waiting, even in ignorance, is to advance unconsciously, because it is God you are dealing with, and He is working in you. God, who calls you to wait on Him, sees your weak efforts, and uses it in you. Your spiritual life is in no respect your own work; as little as you began it, can you continue it. It is God's Spirit who has begun the work in you of waiting on God. He will enable you to wait continually.

Waiting continually will be honored and rewarded by God himself working continually. We are coming to the end of our meditations. It is vitally important that you and I learn one lesson: God must, God will work continually. He works continually, but the experience of it is blocked by unbelief. But He, who by His Spirit teaches you to wait continually, through waiting will also bring you to experience His work. In the love and the life and the work of God there can be no break, no interruption.

Do not limit God in this by your thoughts of what may be expected. Fix your eyes on this one truth: in His very nature, God, as the only giver of life, *cannot do otherwise than every moment work in His child*. Do not look only at the one side: "If I wait continually, God will work continually." No, look also at the other side. Place God first and say, *"God works continually; every moment I may wait on Him continually."* Take time until the vision of your God working continually, without one moment's intermission, fills your being. Your waiting continually will then come naturally. Full of trust and joy, the holy habit of the soul will be: "On thee do I wait *all the day*." The Holy Spirit will keep you always waiting.

My soul, wait only on God!

MOMENT BY MOMENT

I the Lord do keep it: I will water it every moment.

Dying with Jesus, by death reckoned mine;
Living with Jesus, a new life divine;
Looking to Jesus till glory doth shine,
Moment by moment, O Lord, I am Thine.

Chorus:
    Moment by moment I'm kept in His love;
    Moment by moment I've life from above;
    Looking to Jesus till glory doth shine;
    Moment by moment, O Lord, I am Thine.

Never a battle with wrong for the right,
Never a contest that He doth not fight;
Lifting above us His banner so white,
Moment by moment I'm kept in His sight.

Never a trial that He is not there,
Never a burden that He doth not bear,
Never a sorrow that He doth not share,
Moment by moment I'm under His care;

Never a heartache, and never a groan,
Never a teardrop and never a moan;
Never a danger but there on the throne,
Moment by moment He thinks of His own.

Never a weakness that He doth not feel,
Never a sickness that He cannot heal;
Moment by moment, in woe or in weal,
Jesus, my Saviour, abides with me still.

31

Only on God

"*My soul, wait thou only upon God; for my expectation is from him. He only is my rock and my salvation*" (Ps. 62:5, 6).

It is possible to be waiting continually on God, but not *only* on Him. There may be other secret confidences that get in the way and prevent the expected blessing. And so the word *only* must throw its light on the path to the fullness and certainty of blessing. "My soul, wait thou *only* upon God. . . . He *only* is my rock."

Yes, "my soul, wait thou only upon God." There is only one God, one source of life and happiness for the heart: "He *only* is my rock"; "My soul, wait thou *only* upon [God]." You desire to be good. "There is none good but God," and there is no possible goodness except for what is received directly from Him. You have tried to be holy: "There is none holy but the Lord," and there is no holiness except for what He by His Spirit of holiness steadily breathes in you. You would eagerly live and work for God and His kingdom, for men and their salvation. Listen to what He says: "The Everlasting God, the Creator of the ends of the earth. He alone

135

fainteth not, neither is weary. He giveth power to the faint, and to them that have no might he increaseth strength. They that wait upon the Lord shall renew their strength." He only is God; He only is your Rock: "My soul, wait thou only upon God."

"My soul, wait *thou* only upon God." You will not find many who can help you in this. There will be plenty of fellow Christians to entice you to put trust in churches and doctrines, in schemes and plans and human devices, in special ways of receiving grace and special men of God. But, "my soul, wait thou only upon God" himself. His most sacred concessions become a snare when trusted in. The brazen serpent becomes Nehushtan; the ark and the temple a false confidence. Let the living God alone, none and nothing but He, be your hope.

"*My soul*, wait thou only upon God." Eyes and hands and feet, mind and thought, may have to be intently engaged in the duties of this life. "*My soul*, wait thou only upon God." You are an immortal spirit, created not for this world but for eternity and for God. O my soul, realize your destiny. Know your privilege, and "wait thou *only upon God*." Do not let the interest of religious thoughts and exercises deceive you; they very often take the place of waiting on God. "My soul, wait *thou*"—your very self, your inmost being, with all its power—"wait thou only upon God." God is for you, you are for God; wait only on Him.

Yes, "my soul, wait thou *only* upon God." Beware of two great enemies—the world and self. Beware so that no earthly satisfaction or enjoyment, however innocent it appears, keeps you back from saying, "I will go to God, my infinite joy." Remember and study what Jesus says about denying self, "Let a man deny himself." Tersteegen says, "The saints deny themselves in every-

thing." Pleasing self in little things may be stengthen-
ing it to assert itself in greater things. "My soul, wait
thou *only* upon God"; let Him be all your salvation and
all your desire. Say continually and with an undivided
heart, "From him cometh my expectation. He only is
my Rock; I shall not be moved." Whatever your spiritual or physical need is, whatever the desire or prayer
of your heart, whatever your interest in connection with
God's work in the church or the world—as you are alone
or in the rush of the world, in public worship or other
gatherings of the saints, your cry is "My soul, wait thou
only upon God." Let your expectations be from Him
alone. "He only is my [thy] rock."

"My soul, wait thou only upon God." Never forget
the two foundation truths on which this blessed waiting rests. If you are ever inclined to think this "waiting
only" is too hard or too high, these truths will recall
you at once. They are your absolute helplessness and
the absolute sufficiency of your God. Examine deeply
the entire sinfulness of all that is of self, and do not
think of letting self have anything to say for one single
moment. Look closely at your complete and constant
impotence to ever change what is evil in you, or to gen-
erate anything that is spiritually good. Evaluate ever
so carefully your relationship of dependence as creature on God, to receive from Him every moment what
He gives. Let your heart move deeper still into His covenant of redemption, with His promise to restore more
gloriously than ever what you have lost, and by His Son
and Spirit to give within you unceasingly, His actual
divine presence and power. And thus wait on your God
continually and only.

"My soul, wait thou only upon God." No words can
tell, no heart conceive, the riches of the glory of this
mystery of the Father and of Christ. Our God, in the

infinite tenderness and almighty power of His love, waits to be our life and joy. Oh, believer, let it no longer be necessary for me to repeat the words, "Wait upon God," but let all that is in you rise and sing: "Truly my soul waiteth upon God. On thee do I wait all the day."

My soul, wait only on God!

NOTE

My publishers issued a work of William Law on the Holy Spirit.[1] In the Introduction I have said how much I owe to the book. What this author puts more clearly than I have found anywhere else are these cardinal truths:

1. The very nature and being of God, as the only possessor and dispenser of any life there is in the universe, implies that He must continually communicate to every creature the power by which it exists. Therefore He must all the more communicate the power by which a being can do that which is good.

2. The very nature and being of a creature, as owing its existence to God alone, and equally owing to Him each moment the continuation of that existence, implies that its happiness can be found only in absolute, unceasing, and momentary dependence on God.

3. The great value and blessing of the gift of the Spirit at Pentecost, as the fruit of Christ's Redemption, is that it is now possible for God to take possession of His redeemed children and work in them as He did in Adam before the fall. We need to know the

---

[1] *The Power of the Spirit*: A humble, earnest, and affectionate address to the clergy. Out of print; may be difficult to locate.

Holy Spirit as the presence and power of God in us restored to their true place.

4. In the spiritual life, our great need is the knowledge of two great lessons. The one is our entire sinfulness and helplessness—our complete inability by any effort of our own to do anything toward the maintenance and increase of our inner spiritual life. The other is the infinite willingness of God's love, which is nothing but a desire to communicate himself and His blessedness to us to meet our every need, and every moment to work in us by His Son and Spirit what we need.

5. Therefore, the very essence of true religion, whether in heaven or on earth, consists in an unalterable dependence on God, because we can give God no other glory than yielding ourselves to His love, which created us to display in us its glory that it may now perfect its work in us.

I do not need to point out how deep down these truths go to the very root of the spiritual life, especially the life of waiting on God. I am confident that those who are willing to take the trouble of studying this thoughtful writer will thank me for the introduction to his book.